The Great British
Picnic Guide

The Great British
Picnic Guide

Mark Price
'The Chubby Grocer'

EBURY
PRESS

CONTENTS

INTRODUCTION

Picnics have been part of my life for as long as I can remember. They were an exciting and glorious part of my childhood. I still remember the frenzy of the morning before an outing, offering to help but only really getting in my mother's way in the kitchen. But my brother and sister (both younger than me) and I would rely on my father to sort out the biscuits, sweets and pop while we squabbled over sandwich fillings before being packed off into the car by my near-exasperated mother.

As we buckled up and began to play I-spy, my parents packed the car with sandwiches and flasks, home-made fruit cake, apples, bananas and hard-boiled eggs, and occasionally chocolate for a real treat. We would then head off to a local beauty spot, garden, historic monument or wood for an adventure and a picnic. We had picnics throughout the year,

provided the weather was good, and somehow I never remember us complaining about the cold or the damp – we were just so excited to be on an outing.

And while things are very different now for children – they have a greater choice of things to do than we did back then – I have noticed the same element of excitement whenever the idea of a picnic is mooted at home. For it was these warm and loving childhood memories that inspired my wife, Judith, and I to re-invent the family picnic with our two girls, Holly and Lily, who enjoy them as much as we do. We began taking the girls on picnics when they were at toddler stage, so it has become a family ritual that they want as much as we do. The great thing is that they get as excited as I used to.

Throughout the year, often once or twice a month in the summer, we head off in the car, laden with picnic tables and rugs and a veritable feast to a place we all find fun or stimulating. Indeed, choosing the attraction is half the fun, while the food is just as important as the place. Often we simply take our own, but we also hunt down local suppliers, farm shops, child-friendly cafés and pubs serving locally sourced food. And if we don't eat out, we often find goodies to bring home for supper. Picnics have become very much part of our family life and are occasions I love sharing with friends too, which is why I wanted to create this book – as a celebration of the outdoor feast.

I have selected some of our favourite places from all over the country – the beautiful, the unusual, the historic and the quirky. These are some of the places we go back to time and time again. The wonderful thing about this country is that there are so many beautiful locations – parklands, woods, coastal areas, magnificent gardens and great houses – that we can all enjoy. And I think we are particularly lucky to have an organisation such as the National Trust which manages and looks after them so well. This is why I want to play my own small part and donate all my proceeds from this book to the National Trust to help it continue with this great work.

And while I have only listed some of our favourite places, I am sure each reader will have his or her own special picnic spot. I'd like to invite you to share your thoughts and ideas with us, which I can then post on the Chubby Grocer website, so that eventually we will be able to list all the best picnic spots in the UK. Please send your favourites to www.chubbygrocerpicnics.co.uk

Mark Price

The Picnic
A POTTED HISTORY

How did the picnic evolve? Was the very first one, where we ate for pleasure in the outdoors, in the Garden of Eden? Once we'd lost our innocence and were cast out from paradise, eating outside somehow lost its gloss. It seemed that any mention of eating in the open air was for travellers or workers only. Soldiers took rations on their long marches, shepherds took provisions into the mountains, travellers took what they could carry and supplemented their needs en route. The rest of our ancestors remained resolutely indoors.

Indeed, nobody is quite sure when the picnic became the pleasure it is now. In fact, nobody is quite sure where the word came from either. Was it from 'potluck' – a gathering to which each person attending contributed a dish for all to share? Or was it from the French *piquer* – to pick, and its rhyming compatriot *nique* – 'a thing of little importance'. I'd hate to think the French got there first!

Throughout history and literature there are descriptions and illustrations of grand feasts – the dinners at Villa Lante, with its special table along which running water flowed for guests to wash fingers or fruits, the midsummer banquets of Elizabethan England, the glittering garden parties at Versailles. But these were all the prerogative of the rich and noble – the poor might wait at the gate for scraps! And it continued in this vein with the great hunt breakfasts and shooting party lunches of Edwardian England.

However, two events at the end of the 18th century in France and the early 19th century in Britain began to change things. In France after the Revolution, the Royal Parks were opened to the public for the first time and became extremely popular meeting places for the newly enfranchised citizens of the Republic, who used them both to rest and play. And gradually food became an integral part of the hours spent within them.

In Britain, another revolution, the Industrial Revolution, brought people in their thousands to the new centres of industry – dusty, smoky towns and cities. The workers longed for the clean air and space they had left behind, and so

began to plan days out when they could get away from the city to a park, a field, a coastline. From there evolved the picnic we all know and enjoy today – whether it's at the school sports day, on a perfect beach on a sunny summer's day, at a wild and windy point-to-point or an ultra-glamorous event at Royal Ascot's No. One Car Park. Be it on the expansive lawns at Glyndebourne or sheltering from the rain in the wilds of Dartmoor, picnics evoke tastes and memories for all of us.

Perfect Picnics

We always hope for the perfect picnic, and mostly we get it right. But here I have compiled a list of the elements which will help make yours a perfect picnic. I am sure you have even more ideas, in which case it would be great to hear from you. We'd like to post them on the Chubby Grocer website – www.chubbygrocerpicnics.co.uk In the meantime, Happy Picnicking!

Planning is the key

Once you've chosen your location, do a little research. Not just with maps but also read around it. If it has inspired a book, a film, a TV programme, find a copy and get the entire family in the mood by reading or watching it. Better still, if there's a pod cast or a CD that you can play in the car on the way there, it helps get everybody in the mood.

Plot your route, and allow yourself enough time to get to the location of your choice, so that you can enjoy what it has to offer at leisure.

Research local cafés, pubs and farmers' markets, so that if you wish, you can add to your picnic, enjoy a meal you haven't prepared, or have a back-up plan just in case the weather changes.

Picnic equipment

● We prefer rugs (the ones with the waterproof linings) to folding chairs, but if the latter is your choice, make sure they are sturdy and fold easily. The same applies to a picnic table.

● A large golf umbrella has many uses – a sunshade, a windbreak, as well as the obvious rain shelter.

● Remember you will need to carry your picnic and equipment, so shop around for the lightest and most manageable. Unwieldy old-fashioned hampers full of the family silver and candelabra may look terrific, but their attraction soon fades if you have to take them halfway across Dartmoor. It's better to opt for lighter cooler boxes and bags with plenty of frozen gel packs to keep everything chilled.

● And while china plates and proper cutlery are very grown-up (keep them for Ascot or Glyndebourne), there are now some very well-designed and contemporary-looking plastics which are hard-wearing and don't scratch. However, if there are a lot of you on the picnic, paper plates save on the washing up.

● Make your salad dressing at home and keep in an air-tight container (an old jam jar will be fine, but cover the lid with plastic film to prevent leakage and seepage). Dressing salad leaves just before eating will keep them crisp.

● If, like me, salt and freshly ground pepper are essential to everything you eat, buy a separate set for picnics so that it is kept with all your picnic essentials and you do not leave home without it. Do the same with a bottle opener, can opener and corkscrew. Have a special picnic pack with these essentials in it.

● Paper towels – lots of them – use as napkins as well as to mop up spills, etc.

● A packet of wet wipes (the ordinary as well as the antiseptic variety) – the first for cleansing, the second in case of bites, cuts, etc.

● Take an antiseptic spray too and a simple first-aid kit with plasters, creams, etc.

● Bin liners – one for bio-degradable or recyclable rubbish, one for the rest. Remember, nothing but your footprints should be left behind.

● Binoculars – for bird- and scenery-watching.

Safety hints
● Make sure all plates, cutlery, serving bowls and storage boxes are spotlessly clean before setting out.

● Separate foodstuffs – salad leaves in one container, cooked meats in another, cheeses in a third.

● Keep all serving bowls covered at all times to keep insects as well as dust at bay. Many containers come with covers, or you can buy muslin covers for all sized bowls and containers.

● Don't take perishable foods like creams, mayonnaises and ice creams out of the cooler boxes until the last minute.

● Wash your hands with either an antiseptic dry hand wash or an antiseptic wet wipe before you begin to serve the food.

● Always make sure barbecuing is allowed in your chosen picnic site – they may be prohibited for safety reasons.

● If barbecuing, make sure that all raw meats are separate from the other ingredients and are cooked until the juices run clear when pierced in the middle. Just because meat looks charred from the outside, it doesn't follow that it is cooked all the way through.

● Don't put raw chicken or meat next to cooked food on the barbecue.

● Never add sauces or marinades to cooked food if they have been used with raw chicken or meat.

● Use separate tongs and servers for raw and cooked foods.

● If your barbecue is the disposable type, always make sure it is fully extinguished before throwing it away.

Sandwiches & Wraps

Hummus, Corn and Beetroot Wrap Pitta Pockets Mediterranean Picnic Bread **Ciabatta with Olives and Anchovies** Seafood Pan-bagnat Crab, Lime and Coriander Open Sandwich **Chicken and Garlic Mayo Wraps** Bacon and Avocado Rolls Prosciutto, Porcini and Olive Schiacciata **Sausage and Roasted Onion Baguettes**

Hummus, Corn and Beetroot Wrap

SERVES: 4
Preparation time: 5 minutes
Total time: 5 minutes

4 soft tortilla wraps
8 tbsp hummus
4 spring onions, finely chopped
4 tbsp canned sweetcorn, drained
4 small cooked beetroot, sliced and drained
Freshly ground black pepper

Soften the tortilla wraps by placing them in a dry pan over a low heat. Place each one on a board and spread 2 tbsp of the hummus onto each one in a thick line down the centre.

Top each one with a spring onion, 1 tbsp of sweetcorn and a beetroot then season to taste. Roll up each tortilla and wrap each one individually in plastic film, foil or baking paper for transporting.

Pitta Pockets

SERVES: 4
Preparation time: 10 minutes
Total time: 10 minutes

4 pitta breads, toasted
Handful of watercress
2 vine-ripened tomatoes, sliced
150 g (5½ oz) Gruyère cheese, sliced

Cut each pitta bread in half crossways then open up each half to make a pocket.

Fill each pocket with some watercress, plus a few slices of tomato and Gruyère. Wrap each pitta pocket in plastic film.

We often wrap our sandwiches in greaseproof paper
– I always think they get less soggy that way!

Mediterranean Picnic Bread

MAKES: I LOAF (8 PORTIONS)
Preparation time: 45 minutes,
plus rising and proving
Cooking time: 45 minutes
Total time: I hour 30 minutes,
plus rising and proving

400 g (14 oz) strong white bread flour, plus extra for dusting
7 g sachet fast-action dried yeast
4 sprigs fresh rosemary, stalks removed and leaves finely chopped
I tsp salt
4 tbsp chilli oil
Sunflower oil, for greasing
225 g (8 oz) chorizo, skin removed and thinly sliced
I red onion, thinly sliced
75 g (3 oz) pine nuts, lightly toasted
150 g (5½ oz) sun-dried tomatoes in oil, drained well and roughly chopped

To make the dough, mix together the flour, yeast, rosemary and salt in a large bowl. Make a well in the centre and add 3 tbsp of the chilli oil and 250 ml (9 fl oz) warm water. Using a round-bladed knife, mix the ingredients to form a soft dough. If the dough feels dry, add a little more water, sparingly.

Turn out onto a lightly floured surface. Knead the dough using the heel of your hand to stretch it out then fold it in half; continue this process for about 10 minutes until it is smooth and elastic. Place in a large, lightly oiled bowl. Cover with plastic film and leave in a warm place for about I hour until the dough has doubled in size.

Heat the remaining chilli oil over a medium heat in a frying pan and fry the chorizo along with the onion and pine nuts for about 3 minutes, until they just start to colour. Leave to cool completely.

Using a floured hand, punch the risen dough to knock out the air bubbles. Place on a lightly floured surface, knead gently then roll out to a 30 cm (12 in) square. Spread with the sausage and onion mixture so the ingredients are evenly dispersed. Scatter over the chopped tomatoes.

Grease a loose-bottom, 23 cm (9 in) round cake tin. Roll up the dough, Swiss roll-style, so that the filling is enclosed. Using your hands, gently squeeze the dough to elongate it until it measures about 50 cm (20 in) in length then, with a lightly floured, sharp knife, slice the dough roll into 8 equal pieces.

Arrange the dough, cut ends facing up, in the greased tin, spacing them out evenly. The dough will rise during proving to fill any gaps. Cover with a piece of oiled plastic film and leave in a warm place, such as an airing cupboard, for about 45 minutes until the dough has risen to the top of the tin.

Preheat the oven to 200°C, gas mark 6. Bake for 35–40 minutes until golden. Remove from the tin and cool on a wire rack. When cool, wrap in foil or plastic film. Tear into portions to serve – there is no need for a knife.

Ciabatta with Olives and Anchovies

SERVES: 8
Preparation time: 5 minutes
Total time: 5 minutes

1 ciabatta loaf
Black olive tapenade, for spreading
6–10 anchovy fillets
3–4 vine-ripened tomatoes, sliced
Handful basil

Split the ciabatta in half lengthways and spread a layer of tapenade on one half.

Arrange the anchovies, tomatoes and basil on top of the tapenade.

Place the other half of the loaf on top and press firmly together. Wrap in plastic film to transport then cut into slices to serve.

Seafood Pan-bagnat

SERVES: 4
Preparation time: 30 minutes, plus
overnight setting
Cooking time: 15 minutes
Total time: 45 minutes, plus
overnight setting

1 round wholemeal loaf, about 400 g (14 oz) total
175 g (6 oz) butter
300 g (10½ oz) peeled raw tiger prawns
450 g (1 lb) salmon fillets
1 garlic clove, crushed
1 red chilli, seeded and finely chopped
Handful fresh coriander, finely chopped
Finely grated zest of 1 lemon
1 tsp cumin seeds
15 mint leaves, finely chopped
½ tsp paprika
Salt and freshly ground black pepper

Pre-heat the oven to 200°C, gas mark 6. Using a bread knife, cut a horizontal slice from the top of the loaf and reserve. Using a small serrated knife, cut out the centre of the loaf to leave a case, about 1 cm (½ in) thick. Use a spoon to scoop the bread from inside the loaf (reserve this to make breadcrumbs, if you like). Try not to make any holes in the crust for the filling to seep through.

Melt 25 g (1 oz) of the butter and brush it over the insides of the 'case' and the 'lid'. Place both on a baking sheet and bake for 10 minutes until pale golden. Leave to cool.

Dry the prawns on kitchen paper. Place the fish fillets in a heavy-based frying pan and add 4 tablespoons water. Cover and cook gently for 6–8 minutes until the fish is opaque and cooked through. Transfer to a plate and leave to cool. Rinse and dry the pan then melt a further 15 g (½ oz) of the butter. Add the prawns and fry gently for 3 minutes until evenly pink, turning once. Transfer to a plate and leave to cool.

Cut the remaining butter into pieces and place in the pan with the garlic, chilli, coriander, lemon zest, cumin, mint and paprika. Heat very gently, stirring, until the butter has melted and the ingredients are evenly mixed.

Roughly flake the fish, discarding the skin and checking the flesh for stray bones. Pack half into the bread case and add half the prawns. Pour a third of the butter mixture over. Add the rest of the fish and prawns and pour the remaining butter over. Season each layer. Position the lid on top and leave to cool.

Wrap the loaf firmly in plastic film and chill until the butter has set (make it the day before serving and chill overnight). Transport in a rigid container, taking a board and bread knife for cutting the loaf into chunky slices. Take plenty of lemon or lime wedges for squeezing over and a jar of mayonnaise or hollandaise sauce to serve.

Crab, Lime and Coriander Open Sandwich

SERVES: 2–4
Preparation time: 5 minutes
Total time: 5 minutes

2 tbsp mayonnaise
Juice of 1 lime
3 tbsp chopped fresh coriander, plus extra to serve
200 g (7 oz) white crabmeat
Freshly ground black pepper, to taste

TO SERVE:
4 slices rye bread with sunflower seeds
16 thin slices cucumber

Mix the mayonnaise with the lime juice, coriander and crabmeat until combined then season with pepper. Transfer to an airtight container and keep cool until ready to serve.

When ready to serve, spoon the crab mixture on top of the slices of rye bread and top with the cucumber and extra coriander, if using.

Chicken and Garlic Mayo Wraps

SERVES: 4
Preparation time: 5 minutes
Total time: 5 minutes

1 small clove garlic, crushed
2 tbsp mayonnaise
4 tortilla wraps
2 cooked chicken breast fillets
2 tbsp pine nuts, toasted
4 Little Gem lettuce leaves
Salt and freshly ground black pepper

Mix together the garlic and mayonnaise and spread over the tortillas, leaving a gap around the edge.

Slice the chicken breast fillets and divide between the wraps, placing the slices down the centre.

Sprinkle the pine nuts over the top, season and top with the Little Gem lettuce. Roll each tortilla tightly, cut in half, and wrap in plastic film.

This is one of our favourites. On a very cold winter's day or nice summer's day I barbecue the chicken to give it extra flavour. Lovely!

Bacon and Avocado Rolls

SERVES: 2
Preparation time: 5 minutes
Cooking time: 10 minutes
Total time: 15 minutes

4 rashers bacon
1/2 avocado, stoned and peeled
Squeeze of lemon juice
2 ciabatta rolls
1–2 tbsp mayonnaise
2 lettuce leaves
Salt and freshly ground black pepper

Pre-heat the grill to medium-high then grill the bacon until crisp. Mash the avocado and add a squeeze of lemon juice to prevent it discolouring.

Cut the rolls in half, spread each with the mayonnaise then top with the mashed avocado and bacon followed by a lettuce leaf. Season to taste then wrap for transporting.

Prosciutto, Porcini and Olive Schiacciata

SERVES: 4
Preparation time: 40 minutes, plus
rising and proving
Cooking time: 40 minutes
Total time: 1 hour 20 minutes, plus
rising and proving

30 g (1½ oz) dried porcini mushrooms
350 g (12 oz) strong white flour, plus extra for dusting
7 g sachet fast-action dried yeast
50 g (2 oz) Parmesan, finely grated
3 tbsp extra-virgin olive oil, plus extra for greasing
80 g (5 oz) prosciutto, torn into pieces
14 pitted black olives, chopped
125 g (4½ oz) ricotta cheese
1 long sprig rosemary, leaves removed from the stalk in small sprigs
Salt and freshly ground black pepper

Place the mushrooms in a small bowl, cover with boiling water and leave to stand for 20 minutes. Drain well then roughly chop.

Place the flour, yeast, Parmesan, porcini and a pinch of salt in a mixing bowl. Add the olive oil and 200 ml (7 fl oz) hand-hot water. Mix until it becomes a soft dough, adding a little more hot water if necessary.

Turn out the dough onto a floured surface and knead for 5–10 minutes until it is smooth and elastic. Transfer the dough to a lightly oiled bowl, cover with plastic film and leave in a warm place for about 1 hour, or until doubled in size.

Pre-heat the oven to 200°C, gas mark 6. Lightly oil the base and sides of a 23 cm (9 in) round springform tin. Cut the dough in half and roll out each piece to a 23 cm (9 in) round. Place 1 round in the tin, pressing it to fit. Scatter half the prosciutto and olives over the dough. Place the second layer of dough on top.

Pierce the dough all over with a fork and scatter the surface with the remaining prosciutto and olives.

Dot with teaspoonfuls of the ricotta and scatter with the rosemary. Drizzle with a little olive oil and season generously with black pepper. Cover with lightly oiled plastic film and leave in a warm place for a further 30 minutes.

Bake for 40 minutes or until the dough is risen and golden. Leave to cool then remove from the tin and transfer to a board or platter; cover with foil. Pack a knife for cutting the bread into wedges.

Sausage and Roasted Onion Baguettes

SERVES: 6
Preparation time: 5 minutes
Cooking time: 30 minutes
Total time: 35 minutes

12 pork sausages
3 red onions, cut into wedges
6 small baguettes

FOR THE SAUCE:
1 tbsp sunflower or vegetable oil
2 tbsp tomato ketchup
1 tbsp clear honey
1 tbsp dark muscovado sugar
2 tbsp soy sauce

Pre-heat the oven to 220°C, gas mark 7. Line a large roasting tin with baking paper. Place the sausages and onion wedges in the tin.

In a small bowl, mix together all the ingredients for the sauce and drizzle it over the sausages and onions, turning to coat them well.

Place the roasting tin in the oven. Bake for 25–30 minutes, turning the sausages and onions occasionally until cooked through and browned.

Split the baguettes in half horizontally and fill with the sausages and onions. Spoon any sauce left in the bottom of the tin over the filling.

Finger Food & Other Savoury Dishes

Picnic Empanadas   Spinach, Parmesan and Spaghetti Frittata   Summer Pea & Mint Soup   Goats' Cheese with Basil and Sweet Chilli Sauce   Leek and Cheddar Tart Spanish Vegetable Tortilla   Spicy Pea Patties with Tzatziki Goats' Cheese and Pesto Tart   Vegetable and Feta Parcels Orchard Fruit Chutney   Roasted Squash Koftas Parmesan Twists   Caramelised Onion Tart with Gruyère Sesame Cheese Biscuits   Poached Salmon with Watercress   Salmon and Leek Burgers   Hot-smoked Trout and Leek Frittata   Simple Crab Pâté   Chinese Chicken Drumsticks   Roasted Chicken and Potatoes with Orange and Chilli   Cheesy Ham Pasties   Pizzettes Sausage Rolls with Cranberries and Sage   Roasted Honey-glazed Gammon   Bacon and Pea Quiche Barbecue Spare Ribs   Italian Picnic Pasties   Marinated Beef with Roasted Cherry Tomatoes

Picnic Empanadas

MAKES: 18
Preparation time: 15 minutes
Cooking time: 30 minutes
Total time: 45 minutes

25 g (1 oz) butter
1 onion, finely chopped
1 large sweet potato, about 250 g (9 oz), peeled and finely diced
1 tsp ground paprika
1 tsp ground cumin
Handful coriander leaves, finely chopped
500 g (1 lb 2 oz) puff pastry
Plain flour, for dusting
1 medium egg, beaten
Salt and freshly ground black pepper

Preheat the oven to 200°C, gas mark 6. Melt the butter in a frying pan, then add the onion and cook over a low heat for about 10 minutes until golden and very soft.

Add the sweet potato, paprika and cumin then cook, stirring, over a medium heat for 2–3 minutes. Season and stir in the coriander. Leave to cool for about 5–10 minutes.

Meanwhile, roll out the pastry on a lightly floured surface to a 3 mm (1/8 in) thickness, then cut out about 18 rounds, using a 10 cm (4 in) cutter or upturned cup.

Spoon a little of the filling onto one side of each round and brush the edges with beaten egg. Fold over to form a crescent shape and pinch the edges together firmly.

Place on a non-stick baking sheet, brush with egg and cook for 10–15 minutes until well risen and golden.

Allow to cool on a wire rack or wrap in baking paper and a layer of foil to keep warm for the picnic.

Spinach, Parmesan and Spaghetti Frittata

SERVES: 4–6
Preparation time: 10 minutes
Cooking time: 45 minutes
Total time: 55 minutes

Butter, for greasing
6 medium eggs
200 ml (7 fl oz) milk
200 g (7 oz) mature Cheddar, grated
50 g (2 oz) Parmesan, grated
250 g (9 oz) baby spinach, trimmed, blanched, drained and chopped
6 spring onions, finely sliced
200 g (7 oz) cooked spaghetti, roughly chopped (or any cooked, leftover pasta)
Salt and freshly ground black pepper

Pre-heat the oven to 200°C, gas mark 6. Lightly grease a 23 cm (9 in) round or 20 cm (8 in) square flan dish or a deep, ovenproof frying pan with melted butter.

In a large bowl, whisk together the eggs and milk. Add the Cheddar, Parmesan, spinach and spring onions. Mix well and stir in the cooked pasta. Season and pour into the prepared dish or pan.

Bake, covered, for 40–45 minutes or until the frittata is set and browned on top.

Wrap in foil then serve cut into squares or wedges.

Summer Pea and Mint Soup

SERVES: 4–6

Preparation time: 10 minutes, plus chilling

Cooking time: 20 minutes

Total time: 30 minutes, plus chilling

1 tsp butter
2 cloves garlic, chopped
1 large leek, thinly sliced
250 g (9 oz) courgettes, thinly sliced
3 sprigs fresh basil
250 g (9 oz) peas, fresh or frozen
700 ml (1¼ pints) hot chicken or vegetable stock
20 g (¾ oz) fresh mint, roughly chopped
500 g (1 lb 2 oz) Greek yoghurt
Salt and freshly ground black pepper
Ice cubes, to serve

Melt the butter in a large saucepan then add the garlic and leek. Fry for 4 minutes until the leek is translucent. Stir in the courgettes and basil sprigs and cook for a further 5 minutes, until the courgettes are softened but not coloured.

Add the peas and then pour in the stock. Bring to the boil, cover, and simmer for 10 minutes. Turn off the heat, allow to cool then remove and discard the basil.

Stir the mint and Greek yoghurt into the cooled soup then, using a hand-held blender or food processor, blend until completely smooth. Season to taste, and then chill for 2 hours or until ready to transport.

Add a few cubes of ice to a large flask then pour in the soup to keep it cool.

Goats' Cheese with Basil and Sweet Chilli Sauce

SERVES: 8
Preparation time: 10 minutes

6 tbsp sweet chilli dipping sauce
2 x 150 g tubs soft goats' cheese
Handful basil leaves
1 red chilli, seeded and finely chopped (optional)

TO SERVE:
Crudités, such as radishes, carrots, cucumber and celery
Cheese biscuits, such as oatcakes

Prepare the crudités then place them in a plastic food bag, seal and chill. Keep the sweet chilli dipping sauce and goats' cheese in their packaging until ready to serve.

To assemble the dish, turn out the goats' cheese onto a platter and drizzle with the sweet chilli dipping sauce. Remove the basil leaves from their stalks and tear into small pieces if large. Sprinkle the basil over the goats' cheese, followed by the chilli, if using.

Serve immediately with the selection of prepared crudités and your favourite cheese biscuits, such as oatcakes.

The girls really love eating this moreish dip with tortilla chips – the Waitrose ones are particularly good!

Leek and Cheddar Tart

SERVES: 6

Preparation time: 20 minutes,
plus chilling

Cooking time: 50 minutes

Total time: 1 hour 10 minutes,
plus chilling

Butter, for greasing
500 g (1 lb 2 oz) ready-made shortcrust pastry
Plain flour, for dusting
1 tbsp olive oil
5–6 medium leeks, trimmed, washed and sliced
3 large eggs
4 tbsp finely chopped chives or oregano
2 tbsp clear honey
250 g (9 oz) half-fat crème fraîche
125 g (4½ oz) mature Cheddar, grated
Salt and freshly ground black pepper

Pre-heat the oven to 200°C, gas mark 6. Grease a deep 24 cm (9½ in) diameter fluted tart tin and place on a baking sheet.

Roll out the pastry on a lightly floured surface slightly larger than the tin. Carefully lift the pastry into the tin and gently press it into the base and sides. Trim any excess pastry and prick the base with a fork. Chill in the fridge for 20 minutes.

Heat the oil in a large frying pan and gently cook the leeks for 5–8 minutes until wilted and softened, but not too coloured. Remove from the heat and leave to cool.

When the pastry is chilled, place a sheet of baking paper on top of it, scrunching the edges to fit. Fill with baking beans, dried beans or rice grains to weigh down the pastry and stop it from rising while it is being part-cooked. Bake in the oven for 15 minutes.

Meanwhile, place the eggs in a bowl and beat with the chives, honey and crème fraîche. Season then add the cooled leeks and mix well. Stir the Cheddar into the egg mixture.

Remove the baking beans and baking paper from the pastry

shell and pour the egg mixture into the base. Bake for 35 minutes until lightly golden and set. Don't worry if it still has a slight wobble as it will continue to cook for a while when removed from the oven and set further as it cools. When cold, wrap in foil then cut into wedges and serve with a green salad, if liked.

Spanish Vegetable Tortilla

SERVES: 4–6
Preparation time: 10 minutes
Cooking time: 45 minutes
Total time: 55 minutes

3 tbsp olive oil
2 onions, sliced
2 potatoes, about 600 g (1 lb 5 oz), peeled and thinly sliced
200 g (7 oz) frozen petit pois
6 large eggs
Salt and freshly ground black pepper

Heat 2 tablespoons of the oil in a 20 cm (8 in) lidded frying pan with a heat-resistant handle. When hot, add the onions and potatoes and stir to coat them in the oil. Season then reduce the heat to low. Cover and cook gently for 15 minutes, turning the vegetables occasionally from time to time, until they have softened. Remove from the pan and set aside on a plate.

Tip the peas into the pan, increase the heat slightly and stir-fry for 1 minute until starting to soften. Beat the eggs together lightly in a large bowl and season well. Stir the potatoes, onions and peas into the eggs and mix thoroughly. Return the pan to the heat and add the remaining oil. When hot, pour in the egg mixture and reduce the heat to low. Cook for 20–25 minutes, without stirring, until there is virtually no raw egg left on the surface.

Preheat the grill to high. Place the pan under the grill for 2–3 minutes until the tortilla is set and golden brown. Leave to cool before cutting into wedges or wrap in foil until ready to serve.

Spicy Pea Patties with Tzatziki

MAKES: 24
Preparation time: 20 minutes
Cooking time: 15 minutes
Total time: 35 minutes

250 g (9 oz) frozen petit pois or peas
I tbsp olive oil
I onion, finely chopped
I tsp ground cumin
I tsp sesame seeds
I red chilli, seeded and finely chopped
20 g (³/₄ oz) fresh coriander, chopped
I medium egg
50 g (2 oz) fresh breadcrumbs
Plain flour, for dusting
Vegetable oil, for shallow frying

FOR THE TZATZIKI:
I medium courgette, finely grated
2 garlic cloves, crushed
4 tbsp finely chopped mint
200 g (7 oz) Greek yoghurt
Salt and freshly ground black pepper

To make the tzatziki, mix all the ingredients together in a jar or a container with a lid; season and chill.

Place the petit pois in a large bowl and cover with boiling water from the kettle. Leave to stand for a minute, then drain well in a colander. If using peas then cook according to the instructions on the pack.

Heat the olive oil in a small frying pan and gently cook the onion for 3 minutes until beginning to soften. Stir in the ground cumin, sesame seeds and chilli, and cook for a further 2–3 minutes.

Place the onion mixture in a food processor with the drained peas and blitz for a few seconds until coarsely ground. Add the coriander and egg, and blitz again until evenly combined (the mixture should resemble a thick, coarse paste). Stir in the breadcrumbs and season well.

Take teaspoons of the mixture and, with floured hands, shape them into 24 small balls, and then flatten them slightly into discs.

Gently heat about 2 cm (³/₄ in) of vegetable oil in a deep-sided frying pan. Drop a little of the mixture into the oil to test if it is hot enough. If it sizzles and browns, the oil is ready.

Fry the patties in 2–3 batches for 1 minute each side, until golden and crisp on the outside. Remove with a slotted spoon, drain on kitchen paper and allow to cool.
Pack in an airtight container and serve with the tzatziki.

Goats' Cheese and Pesto Tart

SERVES: 4
Preparation time: 10 minutes
Cooking time: 30 minutes
Total time: 40 minutes

500 g (1 lb 2 oz) puff pastry, defrosted if frozen
Butter, for greasing
2 tbsp basil pesto
150 g (5 oz) goats' cheese roll, sliced into rounds
4 vine-ripened tomatoes, thinly sliced
2 tsp dried oregano
Freshly ground black pepper

Pre-heat the oven to 200°C, gas mark 6. Roll out the pastry to a 22 × 30 cm (8½ × 12 in) oblong and place on a large baking sheet. Lightly score a line about 1 cm (½ in) in from the edge of the pastry. (This will form a lip around the tart as the pastry is cooking.)

Spread the pesto evenly over the inner rectangle of the pastry. Place the cheese slices on top then add the tomatoes in an even layer. Scatter with the oregano, and season with pepper.

Bake for 25–30 minutes until the pastry is well risen, golden and cooked underneath. Leave to cool and wrap in foil to transport.

Vegetable and Feta Parcels

SERVES: 2
Preparation time: 15 minutes
Cooking time: 20 minutes
Total time: 35 minutes

1 tbsp olive oil, plus extra for greasing
1 large red pepper, seeded and finely diced
1 courgette, diced
6 spring onions, sliced
1 garlic clove, finely chopped
1 tsp dried oregano
8 small sheets filo pastry
1 medium egg white, lightly beaten
50 g (2 oz) feta cheese, crumbled
Salt and freshly ground black pepper

Pre-heat the oven to 200°C, gas mark 6. Lightly oil a baking sheet.

Heat the oil in a non-stick frying pan and cook the red pepper, courgette, spring onions and garlic for 3–4 minutes until lightly coloured and just beginning to soften. Add the oregano and season well. Allow to cool slightly.

Brush one sheet of filo pastry with a little egg white. Lay a second sheet at right angles over the first and brush with egg white. Continue layering the sheets in this way until you have used four sheets.

Place half the vegetables in the centre of the pastry square and top with half the cheese. Gather up the sides of the pastry to form a 'parcel', press tightly together with your fingers to seal, then place on the baking sheet. Brush with egg white. Repeat with the remaining ingredients to make the second parcel.

Bake the parcels for 12–15 minutes until golden brown. Leave to cool then carefully wrap in foil or put in a plastic container.

Orchard Fruit Chutney

MAKES ABOUT: 1.75 kg
(4 lb 3 oz)
Preparation time: 30 minutes
Cooking time: 1 hour 45 minutes
Total time: 2 hours 15 minutes

75 g (3 oz) fresh root ginger, peeled and finely chopped
1.4 kg (3 lb 4 oz) semi-ripe pears, peeled, cored and chopped
1.4 kg (3 lb 4 oz) Bramley apples, peeled, cored and chopped
2 red onions, chopped
350 g (12 oz) light brown muscovado sugar
2 tsp salt
400 ml (14 fl oz) cider vinegar
1 tsp ground allspice

Put the ginger in a preserving pan or large, heavy-based pan with the pears, apples and onions. Mix in the remaining ingredients and bring the chutney slowly to the boil, stirring frequently.

Reduce the heat to a gentle simmer and let the chutney bubble, uncovered, for about 1½–1¾ hours, stirring frequently, until the chutney has a thick, pulpy consistency. (Wear oven gloves and an apron when stirring the hot chutney, as it is likely to splutter.)

Meanwhile, prepare the jars: first ensure they are free from cracks or chips and pre-heat the oven to 150°C, gas mark 2. Wash the jars in hot soapy water, rinse and dry thoroughly. Place the jars on their sides in the oven for 10 minutes, then turn off the oven and leave until the chutney is ready to pot.

Spoon the chutney into the sterilised jars and cover immediately with spring-clip or screw-top, vinegar-proof lids. Label and store in a cool, dark place for at least 2 months before eating.

Roasted Squash Koftas

SERVES: 6
Preparation time: 15 minutes, plus chilling
Cooking time: 40 minutes
Total time: 55 minutes, plus chilling

750 g (1 lb 10 oz) butternut squash, peeled, seeded and cut into 5 cm (2 in) chunks
1 tsp ground cumin
1 tsp ground coriander
400 g can chick-peas, drained
1 tbsp tahini
1 egg yolk
$\frac{1}{2}$ medium red pepper, seeded and finely chopped
125 g (4$\frac{1}{2}$ oz) mascarpone
150 g (5$\frac{1}{2}$ oz) pistachio nuts, roasted and very finely chopped
125 g (4$\frac{1}{2}$ oz) fresh breadcrumbs
Salt and freshly ground black pepper

TO SERVE
Tzatziki (see page 42)
Green salad

Preheat the oven to 180°C, gas mark 4. Place the squash in a large roasting tin, sprinkle with the spices and season well. Roast in the oven for 30 minutes, until just tender but not coloured. Remove from the oven and allow to cool.

Soak 12 wooden skewers in cold water for 30 minutes to prevent them burning while cooking.

Meanwhile, place the chickpeas and tahini in a food processor and blitz until almost smooth. Add the roasted squash and pulse to form a rough purée. Spoon into a bowl and mix in the egg yolk, red pepper, mascarpone, a third of the pistachios, and all but 4 tablespoons of the breadcrumbs. Season to taste, cover, and chill for 30–40 minutes.

With damp hands, divide the mixture into 12 and shape around the skewers to make koftas, about 17 cm (6½ in) long. Mix the remaining breadcrumbs and pistachios together on a plate. Roll the koftas in the mixture to coat them as evenly as possible.

Prepare the portable barbecue (or preheat a medium grill). Cook the koftas for 4–6 minutes, turning frequently, until golden and hot throughout. If pre-cooking the koftas, leave them to cool then wrap in foil or pack in a lidded container.

Serve with a spoonful of tzatziki (see page 42) and a green salad.

Parmesan Twists

MAKES: 20
Preparation time: 15 minutes
Cooking time: 15 minutes
Total time: 30 minutes

Butter, for greasing
425 g (15 oz) ready-rolled puff pastry (2 sheets)
1 small egg, beaten
2 tbsp finely grated Parmesan
Plain flour, for dusting

Pre-heat the oven to 220°C, gas mark 7, and lightly grease a baking sheet.

Open out the pastry and brush one sheet with egg and sprinkle with Parmesan. Cover with the other sheet of pastry then roll out on a lightly floured surface to a 38 x 25 cm (15 x 10 in) rectangle.

Place the longest edge nearest to you and cut about 20 vertical strips. Twist each one and place on the prepared baking sheet. Bake for 12–15 minutes until crisp and golden.

Allow to cool completely, then pack in a plastic box with scrunched-up kitchen paper on the top to protect them while you are in transit.

Caramelised Onion Tart with Gruyère

SERVES: 6
Preparation time: 10 minutes
Cooking time: 1 hour 10 minutes
Total time: 1 hour 20 minutes

25 g (1 oz) butter, plus extra for greasing
2 red onions, thinly sliced
1 large white onion, finely chopped
375 g (13 oz) ready-rolled shortcrust pastry
Plain flour, for dusting
350 ml (12 fl oz) low-fat crème fraîche
3 medium eggs
Pinch of grated nutmeg
15 g (½ oz) fresh thyme, chopped
150 g (5½ oz) Gruyère, grated
Salt and freshly ground black pepper

Melt the butter in a large pan. Add all the onions and season, then cover and cook gently for 35–40 minutes, stirring occasionally, until they are very soft and starting to caramelise. Remove from the heat and allow to cool slightly.

Meanwhile, pre-heat the oven to 190°C, gas mark 5. Lightly grease a 20 × 30 cm (8 × 12 in) rectangular loose-bottomed quiche tin.

Roll out the pastry on a lightly floured surface and use to line the quiche tin. Line the pastry with baking paper and fill with baking beans. Bake for 15 minutes then lift out the paper and beans and bake for a further 5 minutes until the pastry is light golden.

Place the crème fraîche, eggs, nutmeg and thyme in a large bowl. Season with pepper and whisk together. Stir in the caramelised onions and half the Gruyère, and pour the mixture over the pastry case. Scatter the remaining cheese over the top.

Bake for 30 minutes until the surface is golden and the filling set. Allow to cool before wrapping in foil. Serve with a fresh tomato salad.

Sesame Cheese Biscuits

MAKES: 50–60 BISCUITS
Preparation time: 15 minutes, plus chilling
Cooking time: 10 minutes
Total time: 25 minutes, plus chilling

100 g (3½ oz) mature Cheddar, grated
100 g (3½ oz) butter, softened
100 g (3½ oz) plain flour
1 medium egg yolk
Sesame seeds or poppy seeds, to decorate

Beat together the cheese, butter and flour in a mixing bowl with a wooden spoon, or blend in a food processor for 3–4 minutes until they form a dough.

Roll the mixture into a sausage shape roughly 4 cm (1½ in) thick. Wrap in a square of foil, baking paper or plastic film. Chill in the fridge or freezer for about 1 hour or until firm.

Pre-heat the oven to 190°C, gas mark 5. Line several baking sheets with non-stick baking paper. Slice very thin discs from the chilled (or frozen) dough, and arrange on the baking sheets.

Beat the egg yolk with 1 tablespoon cold water, and then brush the mixture over the tops of the biscuits. Sprinkle with sesame or poppy seeds, and bake for 6–8 minutes until pale golden and slightly risen. Allow to cool on a wire rack.

Poached Salmon with Watercress

SERVES: 8–10
Preparation time: 15 minutes
Cooking time: 5 minutes, plus cooling
Total time: 20 minutes, plus cooling

2–2.25 kg (4 lb 8 oz– 5 lb) whole salmon, gutted and cleaned
1 lemon, thinly sliced
Handful fresh dill
20 g (¾ oz) fresh flatleaf parsley
75 cl bottle dry white wine
300 ml (10 fl oz) fish stock
10 black peppercorns
2 bay leaves, torn
Lemon or lime wedges, to garnish

TO SERVE:
Watercress
Cucumber
Mayonnaise (see page 97)

Poach the salmon up to 24 hours before it is needed. Cool, cover and store in the fridge until ready to use.

Rinse the salmon under cold running water then pat dry with kitchen paper. Fill the cavity of the fish with the lemon slices, dill and parsley. Place the salmon in a fish kettle and pour the wine and stock over, adding a little more wine or water, if necessary, to cover the fish. Add the peppercorns and bay leaves.

Place the fish kettle on the hob and bring the liquid to the boil. Reduce the heat and simmer gently for 5 minutes. Turn off the heat and leave the fish in the poaching liquor to cool completely – at least 2–3 hours.

Remove the cooled salmon from the kettle, drain and place on a tray or large plate. Carefully remove the head, skin and any dark flesh then transfer to a serving platter.

Garnish with lemon or lime wedges and serve with watercress, cucumber and a spoonful of mayonnaise.

Salmon and Leek Burgers

SERVES: 4
Preparation time: 15 minutes, plus chilling
Cooking time: 20 minutes
Total time: 35 minutes, plus chilling

1 leek, finely chopped
1 egg
300 g (10½ oz) hot-smoked salmon, skinned and flaked
Grated zest of 1 lemon and 1 tbsp juice
50 g (2 oz) fresh wholemeal breadcrumbs
Large handful fresh basil, chopped
Olive oil, for brushing
Salt and freshly ground black pepper

TO SERVE:
Wholemeal rolls
Lettuce leaves
Mayonnaise (see page 97)

Steam the leek for 4–5 minutes until tender. Refresh under cold running water, drain, then squeeze out any excess water with your hands.

Place the leeks in a food processor with the egg and blend to a smooth purée. Add all the remaining ingredients, season, and pulse until combined.

Divide the mixture into 4 and, with wet hands, shape into burgers. Brush the burgers with a little oil and chill for 20 minutes.

The burgers can either be grilled for 6–8 minutes each side before the picnic and served cold, or cooked on a portable barbecue.

Serve each burger in a wholemeal roll with lettuce and a spoonful of mayonnaise.

Hot-smoked Trout and Leek Frittata

SERVES: 4–6
Preparation time: 5 minutes
Cooking time: 30 minutes
Total time: 35 minutes

Butter, for greasing
3 leeks, thinly sliced
6 large eggs
100 ml (3½ fl oz) half-fat crème fraîche
2 tbsp chopped fresh tarragon
250 g (9 oz) hot-smoked trout fillets, broken into large flakes
1 tbsp olive oil
Salt and freshly ground black pepper
Mixed leaf salad, to serve

Steam the leeks for about 3 minutes or until tender. Drain and refresh in cold running water, then drain again, squeezing out any excess water with your hands.

Beat the eggs in a large bowl with the crème fraîche and tarragon then season well. Add the leeks and smoked trout and stir gently.

Heat a 20 cm (8 in) frying pan over a medium heat. Add the olive oil and pour the egg mixture into the pan. Cook over a medium heat for 15 minutes. Turn over with the help of a plate and cook for a further 10 minutes until just cooked through. Allow to cool before turning out of the pan. Cut into wedges and serve with a mixed leaf salad.

Simple Crab Pâté

SERVES: 4
Preparation time: 15 minutes, plus
chilling
Total time: 15 minutes, plus chilling

2 tbsp mayonnaise (see page 97)
2 spring onions, finely chopped
1 mild red chilli, seeded and diced
15 g (½ oz) fresh dill, chopped
Grated zest of 1 lemon and 1 tbsp juice
Dash of Tabasco sauce
450 g (1 lb) fresh white and dark crabmeat
200 ml (7 fl oz) crème fraîche
Salt and freshly ground black pepper
Melba toast, to serve

In a large bowl, mix together the mayonnaise, spring onions, chilli, dill, lemon zest and juice, and Tabasco. Season and gently fold in the crabmeat.

Gently fold the crème fraîche into the crab mixture. Divide the mixture between 4 ramekins, then cover and chill in the fridge for 30 minutes.

Cover the ramekins with foil and keep cool until ready to serve with Melba toast.

This is a brilliantly simple starter. We always enjoy it at Lyme Regis or at any other seaside picnic.

Chinese Chicken Drumsticks

SERVES: 6
Preparation time: 5 minutes, plus at
least 15 minutes marinating
Cooking time: 45 minutes
Total time: 50 minutes, plus at least
15 minutes marinating

12 chicken drumsticks

FOR THE MARINADE:
Finely grated zest and juice of 1 orange
2 tbsp clear honey
2 tsp Chinese five spice powder
1 tbsp dark soy sauce
1 tbsp toasted sesame oil

Score the skin on each drumstick twice to allow the marinade to penetrate the meat, then place the chicken in a single layer in a dish.

Combine the marinade ingredients and pour them over the chicken. Turn to coat the chicken in the marinade, then cover and place in the fridge for at least 15 minutes, or up to 24 hours.

Preheat the oven to 190°C, gas mark 5. Tip the chicken and marinade into a roasting tin and arrange the drumsticks in an even layer. Roast in the oven, turning the chicken twice, for 45 minutes until golden and thoroughly cooked, with no pink meat and the juices run clear.

Leave to cool then pack the drumsticks in a lidded container or wrap in foil. Make sure the chicken is kept cold until you are ready to serve.

Roasted Chicken and Potatoes with Orange and Chilli

SERVES: 6
Preparation time: 10 minutes, plus
at least 20 minutes marinating
Cooking time: 30 minutes
Total time: 40 minutes, plus at least
20 minutes marinating

3 tbsp olive oil
1 small red chilli, seeded and finely chopped
2 tbsp sweet chilli sauce
2 cm (¾ in) fresh root ginger, peeled and finely grated
Grated zest of 1 orange, and 2 tbsp juice
6 skinless chicken breast fillets
750 g (1 lb 10 oz) new potatoes, washed and halved
4 sprigs rosemary
Salt and freshly ground black pepper

Pre-heat the oven to 220°C, gas mark 7. In a bowl, make a marinade with 1 tablespoon of the oil, the chilli, sweet chilli sauce, ginger, and orange zest and juice; season well.

Slash each chicken fillet diagonally 4 times, about 1 cm (½ in) deep, and coat with the marinade. Cover with plastic film and marinate in the fridge for at least 20 minutes, or overnight.

Place the potatoes in a large roasting tin. Pour the remaining olive oil over the potatoes and insert the sprigs of rosemary. Season well and bake for 15 minutes.

Turn the heat down to 200°C, gas mark 6. Remove the tray from the oven and place the chicken fillets on top. Spread any remaining marinade over the fillets and return to the oven for 15–20 minutes until cooked. Remove the rosemary sprigs.

Leave to cool then transfer to an airtight container. Keep cool until ready to serve.

Cheesy Ham Pasties

MAKES: 4
Preparation time: 30 minutes, plus chilling
Cooking time: 1 hour
Total time: 1 hour 30 minutes, plus chilling

400 g (14 oz) plain flour, plus extra for dusting
100 g (3½ oz) butter, chilled and cubed
50 g (2 oz) lard, chilled and cubed
75 g (3 oz) mature Cheddar, grated
6–7 tbsp chilled water
Milk or beaten egg, for glazing

FOR THE FILLING:
1 medium potato, about 150 g (5½ oz), peeled and cut into 1 cm (½ in) dice
150 g (5½ oz) swede, peeled and cut into 1 cm (½ in) dice
450 g (1 lb) unsmoked gammon steak, cut into 1 cm (½ in) cubes
1 medium leek, sliced
1 medium onion, sliced
Salt and freshly ground white pepper

To make the pastry, season the flour and sift into a large bowl. Add the butter and lard and rub them into the flour using your fingertips until the mixture resembles fine breadcrumbs. Sprinkle in the cheese and gradually stir in the water (enough to just bind the dough) and draw the mixture together with a round-bladed knife.

Knead the pastry gently on a lightly floured surface until it forms a ball then wrap in plastic film and chill for at least 30 minutes.

Divide the pastry into 4 equal pieces and roll each one out on a lightly floured surface using short sharp strokes, always rolling in one direction. Give the pastry a quarter-turn, then roll it again to form a round about 20 cm (8 in) in diameter and about as thick as a one-pound coin. Cut into a circle using a plate as a guide. Reserve the trimmings to make pastry initials, if you wish.

Pre-heat the oven to 180°C, gas mark 4. Divide the filling ingredients into 4 portions. Arrange a quarter of a portion of potato and swede along the centre of a pastry circle. Top with

the gammon, leek then onion, then the rest of the potato and swede. Season each layer with white pepper.

Lightly brush the edge of the pastry with water then carefully bring up the edges to the centre to cover the filling. Pinch or crimp between the forefinger and thumb of one hand and forefinger of the other to create a sealed crest over the top of the pasty. Add your initials cut from the trimmings.

Repeat with the remaining pastry circles and filling ingredients, place on a baking sheet and chill for 30 minutes.

Brush the pasties with milk or beaten egg and bake for 1 hour until the pastry is golden and the filling cooked through. Leave to cool and wrap in foil for transporting.

Pizzettes

MAKES: 8
Preparation time: 10 minutes
Cooking time: 10 minutes
Total time: 20 minutes

4 ciabatta rolls
8 tbsp passata
1 tsp dried oregano
8 slices Parma ham
2 tbsp pitted black olives, halved (optional)
150 g (5¹/₂ oz) grated mozzarella
Salt and freshly ground black pepper

Pre-heat the oven to 220°C, gas mark 7. Slice the rolls in half horizontally and flatten slightly with the palm of your hand. Mix the oregano into the passata and top each roll half with a spoonful.

Arrange the Parma ham and olives on top, if using, then sprinkle with the mozzarella.

Place on a baking sheet and bake on the top shelf of the oven for 10 minutes, or until the cheese begins to brown. Allow to cool before packing into an airtight container.

Sausage Rolls with Cranberries and Sage

MAKES: 20
Preparation time: 15 minutes
Cooking time: 25 minutes
Total time: 40 minutes

375 g (12$^1/_2$ oz) ready-rolled puff pastry
450 g (1 lb) pork sausagemeat
2 tbsp honey
75 g (3 oz) dried cranberries, roughly chopped
$^1/_2$ tsp dried sage
1 beaten egg, for glazing
Oil, for greasing
Salt and freshly ground black pepper

Pre-heat the oven to 220°C, gas mark 7. Unroll the pastry and cut it in half lengthways.

Place the sausagemeat in a bowl with the honey, cranberries and sage, season well and combine with a fork. Divide the mixture in half and roll each into a long sausage the same length as the pastry.

Place a rolled 'sausage' along one half of the pastry and fold the pastry over to cover the filling completely. Wet the edge of the pastry with a little of the beaten egg and press down firmly to seal. Repeat with the remaining sausage and pastry.

Brush the rolls with beaten egg and cut each one into 10 pieces. Place on a baking sheet and bake for 10 minutes. Reduce the heat to 200°C, gas mark 6, and cook for a further 15 minutes, until the pastry is golden and risen, and the sausagemeat is fully cooked.

Transfer to a wire rack to cool then pack in an airtight container.

Honey-glazed Gammon

SERVES: 8
Preparation time : 10 minutes
Cooking time : 4 hours
Total time : 4 hours 10 minutes

Unsmoked gammon joint, about 2 kg (5 lb 4 oz) total weight
1 large onion, quartered
2 carrots, peeled and halved
2 sticks celery, halved lengthways
4 cardamom pods, lightly crushed
1 red chilli, halved lengthways
1 bay leaf
2 star anise

FOR THE GLAZE:
3 tbsp black bean sauce
2 tbsp set honey
2 tbsp dry mustard powder
Finely grated zest of 2 oranges

Place the gammon in a large pan, keeping the string on to hold the joint together. Add the remaining main ingredients. Cover with cold water, bring slowly to the boil then put on the lid. Simmer for 3 hours, adding extra boiling water from the kettle as needed.

Allow the gammon to cool slightly for 30 minutes in the cooking liquid then place on a board. Reserve the stock for future use and pat the joint dry with kitchen paper. Carefully remove the string, peel away and discard the skin, leaving a layer of fat underneath.

Pre-heat the oven to 220°C, gas mark 7 and place the gammon in a roasting tin. Using the tip of a knife, score the fat with parallel lines to form diamonds. Mix the glaze ingredients together to form a thick paste, and spread over the joint. Roast the gammon for 20–25 minutes until browned and golden.

Rest the joint for 10 minutes before carving into thin slices, or leave the gammon to cool and slice at the picnic. The gammon will keep for up to 3 days in the fridge, wrapped in plastic film.

Bacon and Pea Quiche

SERVES: 8
Preparation time: 10 minutes, plus chilling
Cooking time: 50 minutes
Total time: 1 hour, plus chilling

500 g (1 lb 2 oz) ready-made shortcrust pastry
Plain flour, for dusting
3 rashers smoked streaky bacon, chopped into 1 cm ($^1/_2$ in) pieces
1 small onion, finely sliced
1 garlic clove, finely chopped
225 g (7 oz) frozen petit pois, thawed
3 large eggs
150 ml (5 fl oz) single cream
25 g ($^3/_4$ oz) fresh mint, chopped
Salt and freshly ground black pepper

Preheat the oven to 200°C, gas mark 6. Put a baking sheet in the oven to heat.

Roll out the pastry on a lightly floured surface to a 24 cm (9$^1/_2$ in) circle. Lift into a round 23 cm (9 in) loose-bottomed fluted tart tin, pressing gently into the base and sides. Prick the base with a fork, then chill for 20 minutes while you make the filling.

Heat a large non-stick frying pan and gently cook the bacon for 2–3 minutes until golden. Add the onion and cook for a further 2–3 minutes. Stir in the garlic and petit pois, and toss together well. Remove from the heat and leave to cool.

Place the eggs in a bowl and beat with the cream and mint. Season, add the cooled pea mixture and stir together well. Spoon the mixture into the chilled pastry shell. Bake for 45 minutes. If the top starts to brown too quickly, place a sheet of foil over the top. The surface should be a light golden colour, not too brown.

Leave to cool; it will set further as it cools. The quiche can either be transported in the tin or removed and wrapped well in foil. Serve with a watercress salad.

Barbecue Spare Ribs

SERVES: 4
Preparation time: 10 minutes, plus marinating
Cooking time: 1 hour
Total time: 1 hour 10 minutes, plus marinating

1 kg (2 lb 4 oz) pork spare ribs
3 tbsp clear honey
3 tbsp tomato ketchup
3 tbsp balsamic vinegar
3 tbsp soy sauce

Place the ribs on a large piece of double-thickness foil. In a jug, mix together the honey, ketchup, balsamic vinegar and soy sauce then pour the marinade over the ribs, coating them well. Scrunch up the foil loosely and twist to make a sealed parcel. Marinate in the fridge for 1–2 hours, or overnight if time allows.

If cooking on a portable barbecue, make sure the coals are glowing red under a thin layer of ash. Alternatively, pre-heat the oven to 200°C, gas mark 6.

Place the ribs in the foil on the barbecue or in the oven and cook for 30 minutes. Open up the foil and cook for a further 25–30 minutes until the meat is thoroughly cooked.

You really need to pack extra wet wipes with this dish as fingers will get very sticky!

Italian Picnic Pasties

MAKES: 4
Preparation time: 15 minutes
Cooking time: 20 minutes
Total time: 35 minutes

I garlic clove, thinly sliced
I tbsp olive oil
Plain flour, for dusting
500 g (1 lb 2 oz) puff pastry
4 heaped tsp pesto
250 g (9 oz) mozzarella, drained, patted dry and diced
2 vine-ripened tomatoes, seeded and diced
I beaten egg, for glazing
Salt and freshly ground black pepper
Little Gem lettuce leaves, to serve

Pre-heat the oven to 200°C, gas mark 6. Roll out the pastry on a lightly floured surface to make a 38 cm (15 in) square. Trim the edges then cut the pastry into four equal squares.

Spread each pastry square with a spoonful of pesto, leaving a gap around the edges. Divide the mozzarella and tomatoes between the pastry squares; season. Brush the edges with some of the beaten egg. Pull the corners up to meet in the centre and, using your thumb, press along the edges of the pastry to seal the joins and make neat parcels. Transfer the pasties to a non-stick baking sheet and brush with more egg.

Bake the pasties for 15–20 minutes until risen and golden brown. Leave to cool, wrap in foil and serve with Little Gem lettuce leaves.

Marinated Beef with Roasted Cherry Tomatoes

SERVES: 4
Preparation time: 10 minutes, plus
marinating overnight
Cooking time: 25 minutes (for rare),
plus cooling
Total time: 35 minutes, plus
marinating overnight and cooling

1 large garlic clove, crushed
1 medium red chilli, seeded and finely chopped
2 tbsp grainy mustard
100 ml (3½ fl oz) balsamic vinegar
500 g (1 lb 2 oz) piece fillet steak, topside or top rump
Olive oil, for searing

FOR THE ROASTED CHERRY TOMATOES:
1 tbsp olive oil
600 g (1 lb 5 oz) cherry tomatoes, on the vine
Handful basil leaves
Salt and freshly ground black pepper

Place the garlic, chilli, mustard and vinegar in a shallow dish and mix well. Add the beef, turning to coat it in the marinade. Cover and chill overnight, turning occasionally.

Pre-heat the oven to 200°C, gas mark 6. Remove the meat from the marinade and dry off the beef with kitchen paper. Discard the marinade.

Heat a little olive oil in a large frying pan. Sear the fillet on a high heat until browned all over. Place in a non-stick roasting tin and cook for 25 minutes for rare, 35 minutes (medium) or 40 minutes (well done). Leave to cool, store in the fridge until ready to transport, but serve at room temperature.

Meanwhile, prepare the cherry tomatoes. Put the oil in a roasting tin and add the tomatoes; turn to coat them in the oil. Roast for about 25 minutes until tender. Season to taste. Leave to cool.

To transport, wrap the beef in foil or place in a plastic box. Transport the tomatoes in a separate container and sprinkle with torn basil leaves just before serving.

salads

Roasted Vegetable Salad   Watercress, Carrot, Beetroot and Pine Nut Salad   Apricot and Pistachio Pilaff   Pasta and Broccoli Salad with Watercress Pesto   Moroccan Orange Salad   Summer Pasta Salad   Couscous Salad with Roasted Vegetables   Smoked Mackerel and Bulghar Salad   Vietnamese Chicken Noodle Salad   Ham, Pear and Parmesan Salad   Broad Bean, Ham and Feta Salad   Make Yourself Pasta Salad   Mayonnaise   Saffron Vinaigrette

Roasted Vegetable Salad

SERVES: 4
Preparation time: 15 minutes
Cooking time: 40 minutes
Total time: 55 minutes

1 medium butternut squash, peeled, seeded and cubed
2 red onions, each cut into 6 wedges
2 tbsp olive oil
350 g (12 oz) baby new potatoes, scrubbed
2 tbsp chopped flatleaf parsley
2 tbsp chopped fresh oregano
75 g (3 oz) feta, cubed

FOR THE DRESSING:
3 tbsp extra-virgin olive oil
1 tbsp balsamic vinegar
Salt and freshly ground black pepper

Pre-heat the oven to 200°C, gas mark 6. Put the squash and onions in 2 roasting tins and pour over the olive oil. Turn the vegetables until they are coated in the oil and roast for 35–40 minutes until tender and slightly golden around the edges.

Meanwhile, place the potatoes in a pan, cover with cold water, season with salt and bring to the boil. Reduce the heat and simmer for 10–15 minutes until tender. Drain thoroughly and leave to cool.

Cut the potatoes in half and place in a large lidded bowl with the roasted squash, onions and beetroot, toss gently until combined.

To make the dressing, mix together the extra-virgin olive oil and balsamic vinegar. Season and pour it into a small pot with a lid. Just before serving, dress the salad and scatter the herbs and feta over the top.

Watercress, Carrot, Beetroot and Pine Nut Salad

SERVES: 6
Preparation time: 5 minutes
Total time: 5 minutes

100 g (3 1/2 oz) watercress
1 medium uncooked beetroot, peeled and grated
1 medium carrot, peeled and grated
40 g (1 1/2 oz) pine nuts, toasted

FOR THE DRESSING:
2 tbsp extra-virgin olive oil
Juice of 1 orange
1 tsp balsamic vinegar
Salt and freshly ground black pepper

In a serving bowl with a lid, toss together the watercress, beetroot and carrot.

Place the dressing ingredients in a small jar with a lid, season well and mix thoroughly. Just before serving, drizzle the dressing over the salad, mix again and serve sprinkled with the pine nuts.

Don't forget to share your recipe ideas with me at www.chubbygrocerpicnics.co.uk

Apricot and Pistachio Pilaff

SERVES: 4–6
Preparation time: 5 minutes
Cooking time: 15 minutes
Total time: 20 minutes

25 g (1 oz) butter
1 onion, diced
1 garlic clove, crushed
1/2 tsp ground cinnamon
1/2 tsp ground coriander
250 g (9 oz) basmati rice
500 ml (18 fl oz) hot vegetable stock
75 g (3 oz) ready-to-eat dried apricots, quartered
Handful fresh coriander, roughly chopped
100 g (3 1/2 oz) pistachio nuts
Salt and freshly ground black pepper

Melt the butter in a large, heavy-based pan with a tight-fitting lid. Add the onion and cook for 5 minutes or until golden. Add the garlic, cinnamon and ground coriander and cook for a further minute, stirring continuously.

Pour the rice into the pan and mix well to combine. Add the hot stock and cover. Bring to the boil then reduce the heat and simmer, without stirring, for 10 minutes or until the liquid has been absorbed.

Add the apricots, fresh coriander and pistachios to the hot rice. Season generously, and stir until combined. Leave the rice to cool, transfer to a container with a lid and chill. Keep the rice cold until ready to serve.

Pasta and Broccoli Salad with Watercress Pesto

SERVES: 4
Preparation time: 10 minutes
Cooking time: 15 minutes
Total time: 25 minutes

100 g (3½ oz) watercress, trimmed
50 g (2 oz) feta
Finely grated zest and juice of ½ lemon
50 g (2 oz) pine nuts, toasted
2 tbsp extra-virgin olive oil
400 g (14 oz) penne pasta
200 g (7 oz) small broccoli florets, stalks trimmed
Salt and freshly ground black pepper

For the pesto, blend the watercress and feta in a food processor with the lemon juice, zest and half the pine nuts. Slowly drizzle in the olive oil until almost smooth. Season to taste, then transfer to a bowl and chill.

Bring a large pan of salted water to the boil, add the pasta and cook for 8 minutes then add the broccoli and cook for a further 3–4 minutes or until both the pasta and broccoli are tender. Drain and refresh under cold water. Allow to cool.

To transport, toss the pasta and broccoli in the pesto then place in a plastic container. Sprinkle over the remaining toasted pine nuts before serving.

Moroccan Orange Salad

SERVES: 6
Preparation time: 15 minutes
Total time: 15 minutes

3 large oranges
1/2 pomegranate
60 g (2 1/2 oz) radishes, topped, tailed and thinly sliced
1/2 red onion, finely sliced

FOR THE DRESSING:
2–3 drops orange blossom water (optional)
2 tbsp extra-virgin olive oil
1 tsp clear honey
Large pinch of ground cumin
Salt and freshly ground black pepper

Slice the top and bottom from each orange with a sharp knife. Then follow the contour of each orange to cut away the peel, pith and outer membrane of the fruit in strips (do this over a bowl to catch any juices). Cut each orange horizontally into slices and place on a platter or in a container with a lid. Reserve the juices.

Scoop out the seeds of the pomegranate with a teaspoon. Scatter the seeds over the orange slices, followed by the radishes and red onion.

To make the dressing, place all the ingredients in an empty jar with the reserved orange juice and season to taste. Replace the lid and shake the jar to combine. Transport the dressing in its jar. Shake to re-mix and dress the salad just before serving.

Summer Pasta Salad

SERVES: 4–6
Preparation time: 20 minutes
Cooking time: 15 minutes
Total time: 35 minutes

250 g (9 oz) farfalle pasta
1 tbsp extra-virgin olive oil
1 yellow pepper, seeded and diced
6 spring onions, sliced
400 g can chick-peas, drained and rinsed
Handful basil, chopped
200 g (7 oz) mozzarella, cubed
2 tbsp mayonnaise (see page 97)
Salt and freshly ground black pepper

Cook the pasta according to the instructions on the pack. Drain and stir in the olive oil to prevent the pasta sticking together.

Gently mix all the salad ingredients together in a large bowl with a lid or an airtight container.

Check the flavours and season, if necessary.

Pasta regularly makes an appearance at our picnics. It's easy to prepare, very tasty when cold and is packed full of energy, which is great for the girls as they are capable of burning off plenty of calories.

Couscous Salad with Roasted Vegetables

SERVES: 4–6

Preparation time: 15 minutes, plus cooling

Cooking time: 45 minutes

Total time: 1 hour, plus cooling

175 g (6 oz) couscous

300 ml (10 fl oz) hot chicken or vegetable stock

2 tbsp olive oil

2 courgettes, sliced into 1 cm (½ in) rounds

1 large yellow pepper, seeded and cut into strips

1 large red onion, cut into 8 wedges

100 g (3½ oz) cherry vine tomatoes, halved

2 handfuls rocket leaves

Handful basil leaves, torn

FOR THE DRESSING:

2 tbsp lemon juice

2 tbsp balsamic vinegar

Salt and freshly ground black pepper

Preheat the oven to 200°C, gas mark 6. Place the couscous in a bowl, add the stock and leave for 5 minutes until the water has been absorbed. Fluff up the couscous with a fork and allow to cool completely.

Put the courgettes, yellow pepper and onion in a roasting tin, pour over the olive oil and turn the vegetables until they are coated. Roast in the oven for 35–40 minutes, turning once, until tender and slightly blackened around the edges. Leave to cool.

Place the couscous, roasted vegetables, tomatoes, rocket and basil in a large bowl or container with a lid. Keep cool until ready to serve.

To make the dressing, whisk the lemon juice and vinegar together, season, and store in a pot with a lid. Before serving, pour the dressing over the couscous salad and toss until coated.

Smoked Mackerel and Bulghar Salad

SERVES: 4

Preparation time: 20 minutes

Cooking time: 15 minutes

Total time: 35 minutes

175 g (6 oz) bulghar wheat

50 g (2 oz) watercress, torn into small sprigs

100 g (3½ oz) baby spinach leaves

275 g (9½ oz) smoked mackerel fillets, skinned and broken into large flakes

1 small cucumber, seeded and diced

4 spring onions, sliced

3 vine-ripened tomatoes, seeded and diced

FOR THE DRESSING:

3 tbsp extra-virgin olive oil

2 tbsp horseradish sauce

2 tbsp lemon juice

Salt and freshly ground black pepper

Cook the bulghar wheat following the instructions on the pack. Once cooked, drain if necessary, tip into a large serving bowl with a lid, and allow to cool.

Once cool, stir in the watercress, spinach, smoked mackerel, cucumber, spring onions and tomatoes. Keep the salad cool until ready to serve.

Mix together the ingredients for the dressing in a jar or lidded container; season. Shake the dressing, pour it over the salad and toss until coated.

Vietnamese Chicken Noodle Salad

SERVES: 4
Preparation time: 10 minutes
Cooking time: 8 minutes
Total time: 18 minutes

1 tbsp sunflower oil
400g (14 oz) skinless chicken breast fillets, cut into strips
250 g (9 oz) rice noodles
2 tbsp finely grated fresh root ginger
Juice of 1–2 limes
6–8 tbsp sweet chilli dipping sauce
8 tbsp finely chopped coriander
4 tbsp finely chopped mint
Salt and freshly ground black pepper

Heat the oil in a large frying pan; season the chicken and fry for about 5–6 minutes until cooked through. Leave to cool.

Meanwhile, place the rice noodles in a bowl, cover with boiling water and set aside for 4–5 minutes. Rinse with cold water and drain thoroughly, then return to a serving bowl with a lid.

Add the ginger to the noodles with the lime juice and the sweet chilli dipping sauce, to taste. Season and add the chicken, coriander and mint. Stir gently until combined. Keep cool until ready to serve.

Chinese food is Holly's favourite so over the years we have built a number of Far Eastern flavours into our recipes. This dish is also delicious served hot — I actually prefer it that way.

Ham, Pear and Parmesan Salad

SERVES: 6
Preparation time: 10 minutes
Total time: 10 minutes

18 slices Italian dry-cured ham
2 pears
Squeeze of lemon juice
50 g (2 oz) Parmesan
2 tbsp snipped fresh chives
125 g (4½ oz) baby spinach leaves

FOR THE DRESSING:
2 tbsp olive oil
2 tsp balsamic vinegar
Salt and freshly ground black pepper

To make the dressing, put the olive oil, balsamic vinegar and seasoning in a jar or container with a lid.

When ready to assemble the salad, arrange the spinach then the ham on a platter or in a shallow airtight container.

Quarter and core the pears and then slice thinly. Squeeze the lemon juice over the pears to prevent them browning and arrange on top of the ham. Using a swivel-style peeler, shave wafer-thin slices of Parmesan over the pears and ham.

To serve, shake or whisk the dressing to combine then drizzle it over the salad and sprinkle with chives.

Broad Bean, Ham and Feta Salad

SERVES: 4
Preparation time: 10 minutes
Cooking time: 5 minutes
Total time: 15 minutes

450 g (1 lb) shelled broad beans
2 thick slices ham, diced
100 g (3½ oz) feta, cubed
Handful rocket leaves

FOR THE DRESSING:
2 tbsp extra-virgin olive oil
2 tbsp lemon juice
2 tbsp roughly chopped fresh basil
2 tbsp roughly chopped mint
Salt and freshly ground black pepper

Blanch the broad beans in boiling water until tender then remove the tough outer skin. Allow to cool.

Put the broad beans, ham, feta and rocket in a serving bowl with a lid.

To make the dressing, put all the ingredients in a jar or lidded container for transporting. When ready to serve, shake the dressing and pour it over the salad. Toss the salad until coated in the dressing.

Make Yourself Pasta Salad

SERVES: 4
Preparation time: 5 minutes
Cooking time: 15 minutes
Total time: 20 minutes

350 g (12 oz) penne pasta
Extra-virgin olive oil
Salt and freshly ground black pepper

CHOOSE FROM THE FOLLOWING INGREDIENTS:
1 avocado pear, peeled, stoned and diced
Slices of prosciutto or Parma ham, torn into pieces
Cherry vine tomatoes, halved
Cooked and shelled broad beans
Olives
Diced red pepper
Spring onions
Cooked prawns or chicken
Griddled asparagus
Roasted vegetables
Fresh herbs, such as basil or chives
Sun-dried tomatoes
Parmesan shavings

CHOOSE FROM THE FOLLOWING DRESSINGS:
Extra-virgin olive oil
Mayonnaise (see page 97)
Pesto

Cook the pasta according to the instructions on the pack. Drain, and then cool under cold running water. Drain again.

Transfer the pasta to a shallow bowl or plastic container with a lid. Drizzle with olive oil, season, then stir gently until coated.

At the picnic, allow everyone to select his or her own favourite salad ingredients before mixing them with a dressing in their own bowl or plate.

Mayonnaise

MAKES ABOUT: 125 ML (4 FL OZ)
Preparation time: 15 minutes
Total time: 15 minutes

1 medium egg yolk
1 tsp Dijon mustard
125 ml (4 fl oz) sunflower or groundnut oil
1 tsp lemon juice
Salt and freshly ground black pepper

Place the egg yolk in a medium-sized mixing bowl and add the mustard and some seasoning.

Using an electric whisk or balloon whisk, beat well, then add a drop of oil and whisk until incorporated. Continue adding the oil, drop by drop, until the mixture thickens. (If you add the oil too quickly, the mayonnaise may curdle. If this happens, place a fresh egg yolk in another mixing bowl and add the curdled mixture slowly, as you would the oil. When the mixture becomes smooth again, continue with the recipe.)

Once it has thickened, you can add the oil in a very fine, steady stream. Add the lemon juice and season to taste. Spoon into a jar and chill until needed.

Variations

Try flavouring your mayonnaise with the following suggestions (flavoured mayonnaise should be eaten on the day it is made):
● **Pesto Mayonnaise** – make the recipe as above, then stir in 2 tablespoons fresh pesto.
● **Sweet Chilli Mayonnaise** – make the recipe as above, then stir in 2 tablespoons sweet chilli sauce and a few drops of Tabasco.
● **Mustard Mayonnaise** – replace half of the oil specified above with extra-virgin olive oil, then stir in 1 tablespoon wholegrain and 2 teaspoons Dijon mustard.
● **Herb Mayonnaise** – make the recipe as above, then stir in 2 tablespoons chopped fresh tarragon.

Saffron Vinaigrette

SERVES: 4
Preparation time: 10 minutes
Total time: 10 minutes

One of the most useful of dressings, a vinaigrette is simply a blend of oil and vinegar, measured to give a balance of emollient and sharp flavours. Usually, a piquant ingredient such as mustard or garlic is added, and a vinaigrette should always be seasoned.

A vinaigrette's consistency makes it ideal for clinging to leaves, which is why it's used to dress green salads. But it can be used in all kinds of vegetable dishes, making the ingredients lusciously moist and drawing their flavours together.

Once you know the proportions, you can adapt the basic idea ad infinitum. Work on the ratio of three parts oil to one part vinegar and you can't go wrong. In fact, the beauty of vinaigrette is that it's so easy to correct: if it's too sharp, too oily, or too bland, just add a little more of the appropriate ingredient.

To create your own vinaigrette, try different oils, such as sesame, avocado or walnut. If you use a strong-flavoured oil, such as sesame, dilute it with a light oil such as sunflower, or the result may be overpowering. You can also try different vinegars (cider, balsamic, sherry; not malt) and flavourings, such as tomatoes, herbs or chilli. Match the ingredients to the dish. A warm salad of roasted root vegetables will sing dressed with a robust walnut oil, sherry vinegar and garlic vinaigrette, while green beans and pak choi are delicious bathed in a blend of sunflower and sesame oil, rice vinegar and chilli.

The recipe here infuses a basic vinaigrette with saffron, creating a golden dressing for roasted peppers, or fish, or for a salad of Little Gem, croutons, and diced cucumber and tomato.

Medium pinch of saffron strands
4 tbsp white wine vinegar
6 tbsp extra-virgin olive oil
1 small shallot, very finely chopped
Salt and freshly ground black pepper

Put the saffron and vinegar in a small pan, bring to the boil and simmer for 1–2 minutes until the liquid has reduced to 2 tablespoons. Leave to cool. Put the saffron vinegar in a jam jar, and add the oil, shallot and seasoning.

Put a lid on the jar, and shake hard; you need to mix the liquid vigorously to combine the oil with the other ingredients, and this is one of the easiest ways to do it. Alternatively, you could beat it well with a small whisk then pour into a pot with a lid to store. If left to stand, the dressing will separate, so give it another shake or stir before serving.

Hot Food

Thai Pumpkin Soup Italian Bean and Vegetable Soup
Cannellini Bean and Ham Soup **Hearty Sausage and Barley
Soup** Barbecued Sausages with Fresh Mango Chutney

Thai Pumpkin Soup

SERVES: 4
Preparation time: 20 minutes
Cooking time: 40 minutes
Total time: 1 hour

1 kg (2 lb 4 oz) butternut squash, peeled, seeded and cut into 1 cm ($\frac{1}{2}$ in) cubes
1 tbsp vegetable oil
1 medium onion, chopped
2.5 cm (1 in) piece fresh root ginger, peeled and finely chopped
4 tsp Thai red curry paste
1 stick lemon grass, crushed with the blade of a knife
450 ml (16 fl oz) vegetable stock
400 ml can coconut milk
Juice of 1 lime
Handful basil, chopped
Salt and freshly ground black pepper

Pre-heat the oven to 180°C, gas mark 4. Place the butternut squash in a non-stick roasting tin and season. Roast for 30 minutes or until tender.

Meanwhile, heat the oil in a medium-sized pan and add the onion and ginger. Cover with a lid and sauté for 10 minutes, stirring occasionally. Stir in the curry paste and cook for 1–2 minutes, then add the squash, lemon grass, stock and coconut milk. Cover and bring to the boil, then reduce the heat and simmer for 5 minutes. Remove from heat and cool slightly.

Remove the lemon grass then purée the soup using a hand-held blender until smooth. Season to taste, stir in the lime juice and basil and reheat gently; you may need to add a little more stock or boiling water for a thinner consistency if required.

Pour boiling water into a large flask to warm for 10–15 minutes. Discard the water and pour in the soup, discarding the lemon grass.

Italian Bean and Vegetable Soup

SERVES: 4–6

Preparation time: 15 minutes

Cooking time: 35 minutes

Total time: 50 minutes

3 tbsp olive oil

1 large onion, finely chopped

2 garlic cloves, chopped

40 g (1½ oz) parsley, chopped

1 medium carrot, chopped

2 sticks celery, chopped

1 bouquet garni

3 sprigs fresh rosemary

400 g can chopped tomatoes

1.5 litres (2¾ pints) vegetable stock

1 Savoy cabbage, hard stalks removed and leaves shredded

2 courgettes, diced

400 g can chickpeas, drained and rinsed

Salt and freshly ground black pepper

Heat the oil in a large pan, add the onion, garlic, parsley, carrot and celery and cook gently for 5 minutes or until softened, stirring occasionally. Stir in the bouquet garni, rosemary, canned tomatoes and stock then simmer for 20 minutes.

Stir in the cabbage, courgettes and chickpeas, season, and simmer for a further 8–10 minutes.

Pour boiling water into a large flask to warm for 10–15 minutes. Discard the water and pour the soup into the flask. Pour the soup into mugs or bowls to serve and accompany with plenty of crusty bread and cheese.

Cannellini Bean and Ham Soup

SERVES: 4
Preparation time: 10 minutes
Cooking time: 30 minutes
Total time: 40 minutes

2 tbsp olive oil
1 large onion, chopped
2 sticks celery, chopped
1 large carrot, sliced
2 cloves garlic, finely chopped
1 litre (1³/₄ pints) vegetable or chicken stock
2 x 400 g cans cannellini beans, drained and rinsed
400 g can chopped tomatoes
75 g (3¹/₂ oz) thick ham, cubed
Handful parsley, chopped
Salt and freshly ground black pepper

Heat the oil in a large pan, add the onion, celery and carrot and fry for 7 minutes or until softened. Add the garlic and stock and bring to the boil. Reduce the heat and simmer, partly covered, for 15 minutes or until the vegetables are tender.

Add the beans with the tomatoes, ham and seasoning. Simmer for 5 minutes and then stir in the parsley and serve.

Hearty Sausage and Barley Soup

SERVES: 6
Preparation time: 15 minutes
Cooking time: 50 minutes
Total time: 1 hour 5 minutes

2 tbsp olive oil
2 large red onions, chopped
1 large carrot, sliced
1 stick celery, sliced
2 garlic cloves, finely chopped
250 g (9 oz) chestnut mushrooms, finely chopped
10 good-quality sausages, skin removed
1.5 litres (2³/₄ pints) chicken stock
1 sachet bouquet garni
4 sprigs fresh thyme
100 g (3¹/₂ oz) pearl barley
Salt and freshly ground black pepper

Heat the oil in a large pan, add the onions, carrot, celery, garlic and mushrooms and cook over a medium heat for 5 minutes until softened.

Roughly chop the sausages and add to the pan, stirring well to break them up. Add the stock, bouquet garni, thyme and barley. Season, stir, and bring to the boil. Reduce the heat, cover, and simmer gently for 40 minutes, stirring regularly so that it does not catch on the bottom of the pan.

Pour boiling water into a large flask to warm for 10–15 minutes. Discard the water and pour the soup into the flask. Pour into mugs to serve and accompany with plenty of crusty bread.

Barbecued Sausages with Fresh Mango Chutney

SERVES: 4

Preparation time: 10 minutes

Cooking time: 15 minutes

Total time: 25 minutes

8 good-quality thick sausages of your choice
8 metal or bamboo skewers

FOR THE MANGO CHUTNEY:
1 large ripe mango
2 shallots, finely chopped
3 tbsp red wine vinegar
3 tbsp light brown muscovado sugar
1 tbsp black mustard seeds

Hold the mango firmly on a board and slice down either side of the central stone to remove the 'cheeks'. Place the two sides, flesh-side-up and score a lattice into the flesh. Gently push out the skin from underneath and cut away the cubes. Remove and dice any flesh still clinging to the stone.

Place the mango in a pan with the shallots, vinegar, sugar and mustard seeds. Season, and cook over a medium heat for 15 minutes until tender, adding a splash of water if necessary. Leave the chutney to cool then spoon into a jar or lidded container. This will keep for up to 1 week in the fridge.

If using bamboo skewers, soak in water for about 1 hour to prevent them burning during cooking. Thread the sausages onto 4 pairs of parallel skewers so they look like two rungs on a ladder. Wrap in foil and keep cool until ready to cook.

Preheat the portable barbecue to a medium heat. Barbecue the sausages for 18–20 minutes, turning once, until golden brown and cooked through.

Serve the sausages with the fresh mango chutney.

Cakes, Biscuits & Puddings

Eton Mess   **Plum Crumble Squares with Cinnamon**

Chocolate, Walnut and Date Brownies   **Blueberry, Lime**

and Coconut Slice   Raspberry Custard Fool   Spanish

Almond Torte with Lemon Syrup   **Pimm's Jellies**

Strawberry Bakewell Tart   Cranberry Rock Buns   Apricot

Sponge with Walnuts   **Blueberry Coconut Muffins**   Gluten-

free Date and Pecan Cake   **Gingerbread People**   **Cherry**

and Almond Tart   Pecan Banana Bread   Chocolate

Hazelnut Cookies   Toffee Apple Flapjacks

Eton Mess

SERVES: 4

Preparation time: 25 minutes, plus
cooling

Cooking time: 1 hour 45 minutes

Total time: 2 hours 10 minutes, plus
cooling

3 egg whites
175 g (6 oz) caster sugar
600 ml (20 fl oz) double cream
700 g (1 lb 9 oz) ripe strawberries, hulled and sliced

Pre-heat the oven to 100°C, gas mark 1/2. Whisk together the egg whites and sugar in a large bowl set over a pan of gently simmering water until the mixture forms a thick trail when the whisk is removed.

Carefully remove the bowl from the pan, and continue to whisk for about 2 minutes or until the mixture has cooled down significantly. Using 2 spoons, place 6 meringues onto baking parchment-lined baking trays, then bake for 1 hour 45 minutes. Leave to cool.

Meanwhile, whip the cream until it forms stiff peaks.

When the meringues are cold, roughly crush them and combine with the strawberries and cream. Pile into a serving bowl with a lid. Keep cool until ready to serve.

*This is the perfect picnic pudding
— the messier the better!*

Plum Crumble Squares with Cinnamon

MAKES: 28 SQUARES
Preparation time: 15 minutes
Cooking time: 55 minutes
Total time: 1 hour 10 minutes

450g (1 lb) purple plums, stoned and roughly chopped
200 g (7 oz) caster sugar

FOR THE CRUMBLE TOPPING:
75 g (3 oz) cold butter, cubed, plus extra for greasing
125 g (4½ oz) plain flour
75 g (3 oz) demerara sugar

FOR THE SPONGE:
175 g (6 oz) butter, softened
175g (6 oz) self-raising flour
1 tsp ground cinnamon
3 medium eggs

Pre-heat the oven to 180°C, gas mark 4. Place the plums in a pan with 1 tablespoon of the caster sugar and a splash of water then cook gently on the hob for 5–6 minutes or until just tender. Drain through a sieve, discarding the juice, then leave the plums to cool. Grease a rectangular baking tin, about 27 x 17 cm (10½ x 6½ in) and line the base with baking paper.

To make the crumble topping, place the butter and flour in a food processor and blend until just combined. Add the demerara sugar and pulse a couple of times to give a rough crumble. Remove and set aside. (Alternatively, rub the butter into the flour by hand then stir in the sugar.)

For the cake mixture, mix together the butter, remaining caster sugar, self-raising flour, cinnamon and eggs in a food processor for 30 seconds, or beat with a wooden spoon.

Remove the blade from the bowl and stir in the cooled plums. Spoon the mixture into the prepared tin and sprinkle over the crumble topping, pressing down with the back of a spoon.

Bake for 50–55 minutes or until the sponge has risen and the topping is golden. Remove from the oven, leave to stand for 5 minutes then cool on a rack. Cut into 28 squares just before serving. The cake can be stored in an airtight tin for up to 3 days.

Chocolate, Walnut and Date Brownies

MAKES: 16 SQUARES
Preparation time: 20 minutes
Cooking time: 30 minutes
Total time: 50 minutes

225 g (8 oz) unsalted butter
350 g (12 oz) plain chocolate, at least 70 per cent cocoa solids
4 large eggs
350 g (12 oz) light brown muscovado sugar
1 tsp vanilla extract
225 g (8 oz) plain flour, sifted
200 g (9 oz) walnuts, roughly chopped
100 g (3 1/2 oz) dried dates, roughly chopped

Pre-heat the oven to 180°C, gas mark 4. Grease a 23 x 32 cm (9 x 12 1/2 in) deep-sided baking tray and line with baking parchment.

In a small saucepan, melt the butter and chocolate slowly, stirring regularly. When the lumps of chocolate are fairly small, turn off the heat – there will be enough heat to finish melting the chocolate and you reduce the risk of overheating the mixture. Allow to cool.

In a large bowl, whisk together the eggs, sugar and vanilla extract for 10 minutes or until pale and fluffy.
Stir the chocolate mixture into the egg mixture then fold in the flour, walnuts and dates using a wooden spoon.

Pour the mixture into the prepared baking tray and bake for 25–30 minutes. Test with a skewer; the mixture should seem not quite cooked in the centre. Allow to cool, then cut into 16 squares. Pack in an airtight container.

Blueberry, Lime and Coconut Slice

SERVES 6
Preparation time: 20 minutes, plus
30 minutes cooling
Cooking time: 1 hour 35 minutes
Total time: 2 hours 25 minutes

250 g (9 oz) unsalted butter, cubed, plus extra for greasing
225 g (8 oz) caster sugar
275 g (9½ oz) plain flour, sifted
75 g (3 oz) desiccated coconut
150 g (5½ oz) blueberries
2 large eggs
50 g (2 oz) self-raising flour
Finely grated zest of 3 limes and juice of 2 limes
Icing sugar, for dusting

Preheat the oven to 200°C, gas mark 6. Grease a 17 × 19 cm (6½ × 7½ in) baking tin and line with baking paper that comes 3 cm (1¼ in) above the top of the tin.

Meanwhile, place 125 g (4½ oz) of the sugar in a food processor with the butter, plain flour and coconut. Pulse briefly to combine, then press into the prepared tin and bake for 20–25 minutes until golden. Leave to cool completely.

Spread the blueberries over the cooled shortbread base. Reduce the oven to 170°C, gas mark 3.

To make the lime sponge, beat the eggs with the remaining 100 g (3½ oz) of sugar until thick and pale. Stir in the self-raising flour with the lime zest and juice.

Top the berry-topped shortbread with the lime sponge and bake for 45–50 minutes until the sponge is risen and golden. Allow to cool, and then dust with icing sugar. Transport whole and cut into slices before serving. The slice will keep in an airtight container for up to 1 week.

Raspberry Custard Fool

SERVES: 4
Preparation time: 10 minutes
Cooking time: 15 minutes
Total time: 25 minutes

800 g (1 lb 11 oz) raspberries
2 tbsp caster sugar

FOR THE CUSTARD:
284 ml pot double cream
1 vanilla pod
3 egg yolks
1 tbsp caster sugar
1 tsp cornflour

Place the raspberries and sugar in a pan with a splash of water. Simmer for about 5–7 minutes until thoroughly softened. Press the raspberries through a sieve (or in a blender if you want to include the seeds) and allow to cool.

Make the custard by gently heating the cream and vanilla pod in a saucepan to just before boiling point.

Meanwhile, in a medium bowl, whisk the egg yolks, sugar and cornflour to a smooth paste.

Remove the vanilla pod from the hot cream then reserve to use again. Pour the cream over the paste, whisking all the time. Return the mixture to the pan and cook over a gentle heat, whisking constantly with a balloon whisk. Once the custard has thickened, pour into a bowl to cool.

Mix the cooled custard and puréed fruit together and spoon into a bowl with a lid. Chill then keep cool until ready to serve in bowls or glasses.

Spanish Almond Torte with Lemon Syrup

SERVES: 8
Preparation time: 10 minutes
Cooking time: 45 minutes
Total time: 55 minutes

Butter, for greasing
300 g (10½ oz) whole shelled almonds, skins removed
4 medium eggs, separated
250 g (9 oz) caster sugar
Finely grated zest of 1 unwaxed lemon and 1 tbsp juice
1 tsp ground cinnamon
Whipped cream or yoghurt, to serve (optional)

FOR THE LEMON SYRUP:
Pared and thinly sliced zest and juice of 1 unwaxed lemon
25 g (1 oz) caster sugar

Pre-heat the oven to 160°C, gas mark 3. Grease a 20 cm (8 in) loose-bottomed cake tin and line the base with baking paper. Place the almonds in a food processor and whizz until finely ground.

Place the egg yolks, sugar, lemon zest and juice in a large bowl and whisk with an electric or hand whisk until the mixture becomes thick, creamy and pale. Mix in the almonds and cinnamon.

Place the egg whites in a clean, dry bowl and whisk with a hand or electric whisk until they form stiff peaks. Using a metal spoon, lightly fold 2 tablespoons of the egg white into the almond mixture to loosen it, then fold in the remaining egg white until it is thoroughly combined. Pour into the tin and bake for 45 minutes or until a skewer comes out clean. Leave to cool in the tin.

While the torte is cooling, make the syrup. Reserve a few pieces of lemon zest for decoration then place the remainder with the juice, caster sugar and 1 tablespoon of cold water in a small pan. Heat gently until the sugar has dissolved. Spoon the warm syrup over the top of the torte and leave to cool; decorate with the reserved lemon zest. Just before serving, cut into slices and serve with a dollop of lightly whipped cream or natural yogurt.

Pimm's Jellies

SERVES: 4

Preparation time: 15 minutes, plus
3–4 hours chilling

Total time: 15 minutes, plus 3–4
hours chilling

6 sheets leaf gelatine

6 tbsp Pimm's No.1 Cup, chilled

600 ml (20 fl oz) lemonade, chilled

4 tsp caster sugar

2–4 strawberries, halved

4 thin slices cucumber

4 sprigs fresh mint

Soak the leaf gelatine in cold water for 5 minutes or until soft. Meanwhile, heat the Pimm's until just boiling. Simmer for 10 minutes or until you can no longer smell any alcohol coming off it, then remove from the heat.

Lift the gelatine out of the water, give it a squeeze then stir into the hot Pimm's until dissolved. Add the lemonade and the sugar. Pour through a strainer into a jug.

Pour the jelly into 4 large glasses and chill for 3–4 hours until set. Serve, decorated with the strawberries, cucumber slices and mint sprigs.

Strawberry Bakewell Tart

MAKES: 12 SLICES
Preparation time: 20 minutes,
plus chilling
Cooking time: 30 minutes
Total time: 50 minutes, plus chilling

100 g (3½ oz) unsalted butter, plus extra for greasing
Flour, for dusting
400 g (14 oz) sweet shortcrust pastry
5 tbsp strawberry jam
125 g (4½ oz) caster sugar
3 eggs, beaten
1/2 tsp almond extract
150 g (5½ oz) ground almonds
75 g (3 oz) icing sugar, sifted

Pre-heat the oven to 190°C, gas mark 5. Grease a 30 x 20 cm (12 x 8 in) or 23 cm (9 in) square loose-bottomed fluted flan tin.

Roll out the pastry on a lightly floured surface slightly larger than the tin. Lift the pastry into the tin, pressing gently into the base and sides. Trim the edges and prick the base with a fork then chill for 30 minutes while you make the filling.

Line the pastry case with baking paper and fill with baking beans. Bake for 15 minutes, lift out the paper and beans, and cook for a further 5 minutes until the pastry is light golden. Allow to cool slightly then spread the jam over the base of the pastry. Place the butter and sugar in a medium-sized bowl and beat with an electric whisk until pale and fluffy. Beat in the eggs, a little at a time. Add the almond extract and fold in the ground almonds. Pour this mixture over the jam and level it out with a spatula or the back of a spoon.

Bake the tart on the middle shelf of the oven for 25–30 minutes until cooked and golden. Allow to cool in the tin.

Mix the icing sugar with 1 tablespoon cold water. Drizzle the icing over the top of the tart using a teaspoon. Keep in the tin for transporting, cover with foil, then cut into rectangles before serving.

Cranberry Rock Buns

MAKES: 16 BUNS
Preparation time: 15 minutes
Cooking time: 15 minutes
Total time: 30 minutes

125 g (4½ oz) unsalted butter, slightly softened, plus extra for greasing
250 g (9 oz) self-raising flour
2 tsp baking powder
50 g (2 oz) light brown soft sugar, plus 2 tbsp for sprinkling
100 g (3½ oz) fresh cranberries, quartered
50 g (2 oz) currants
1 large egg, beaten
2 tbsp milk

Preheat the oven to 200°C, gas mark 6. Line 2–3 baking sheets with baking paper or lightly grease with a little extra butter.

Place the flour, baking powder and butter in a mixing bowl and roughly chop the butter with a round-bladed knife. Rub the butter into the flour using your fingertips until the mixture resembles fine breadcrumbs.

Stir in the sugar, cranberries, currants, beaten egg and milk, then use the knife to bring the ingredients together to form a stiff dough. If the mixture is very dry, add a little more milk.

Using a teaspoon, dollop heaps of the mixture onto the prepared baking sheets to make 16 buns, spaced well apart. Sprinkle the remaining sugar evenly over the top of the buns and bake for about 15 minutes until lightly golden brown all over. Cool on a wire rack. Pack the buns in an airtight container. They are best eaten on the day they are made.

Apricot Sponge with Walnuts

SERVES: 8

Preparation time: 20 minutes, plus cooling

Cooking time: 45 minutes

Total time: 1 hour 25 minutes, including cooling

250 g (9 oz) softened butter, plus extra for greasing
250 g (9 oz) caster sugar
4 medium eggs, beaten
1 tsp vanilla extract
100 g (3½ oz) self-raising flour, sifted
100g (3½ oz) shelled walnuts, roughly chopped
200 g (7 oz) ground almonds
250 g (9 oz) Greek yoghurt, preferably 0 per cent fat
400 g (14 oz) canned apricots, drained well and sliced
1 tbsp icing sugar, sifted, for dusting

Pre-heat the oven to 180°C, gas mark 4. Lightly grease a deep 23 cm (9 in) diameter cake tin and line the base with baking paper.

Beat the butter and sugar together in a large bowl until light and fluffy. Gradually beat in the eggs, a little at a time, until fully incorporated and the mixture is smooth. (If the mixture starts to curdle a little, simply add a spoonful or two of the flour and carry on adding the egg.) Stir in the vanilla extract.

Fold in the flour, walnuts and ground almonds. Spoon the mixture into the prepared tin and bake for 40–45 minutes until golden and springy to the touch. Remove from the oven and leave to cool for 10–15 minutes. Turn the cake out onto a wire rack and leave to cool completely.

Cut the cake in half horizontally and spread the yoghurt over the base. Arrange the apricots on top. Sandwich with the remaining cake half and dust the top with icing sugar. To serve, cut into slices using a sharp knife. (The unfilled cake will keep for 1–2 days in an airtight container. Once filled, eat within a day.)

Blueberry Coconut Muffins

MAKES: 20
Preparation time: 15 minutes
Cooking time: 20 minutes
Total time: 35 minutes

284 ml pot buttermilk
200 g (7 oz) light brown soft sugar
75 ml (3 fl oz) vegetable oil, such as groundnut
1 egg
75 g (3 oz) desiccated coconut
1 tsp vanilla extract
2 tsp baking powder
1 tsp bicarbonate of soda
300 g (12 oz) plain flour
150 g (5½ oz) blueberries
Icing sugar, to decorate (optional)

Preheat the oven to 190°C, gas mark 5. Place 20 paper cake cases into 2 x 12-hole bun tins.

Place the buttermilk, sugar, oil, egg, coconut and vanilla extract in a mixing bowl and beat together until well combined.

Sift in the baking powder, bicarbonate of soda and the flour. Use a large spoon to combine very gently. (Don't over-beat the mix at this stage or the muffins will be heavy.)

Add the blueberries and stir gently once or twice to mix. Divide the mixture between the paper cases and bake for 15–20 minutes until well risen, golden and just firm to the touch.

Remove from the oven and allow to cool on a wire rack, then dust with a little sifted icing sugar, if using. Store in an airtight container and eat or freeze on the same day.

Gluten-free Date and Pecan Cake

MAKES: 24 SMALL SQUARES
Preparation time: 15 minutes
Cooking time: 50 minutes
Total time: 1 hour 5 minutes

250 g (9 oz) dates, chopped
150 ml (5 fl oz) boiling water
150 g (5½ oz) butter, softened
100 g (3½ oz) light brown soft sugar
2 tbsp maple syrup
250 g (9 oz) gluten-free plain flour
2 medium eggs, beaten
1½ tsp gluten-free baking powder
1½ tsp mixed spice
50 g (2 oz) pecans, toasted and chopped

Place the dates in a small bowl and cover with the boiling water. Leave until cool and the dates have softened. Meanwhile, pre-heat the oven to 180°C, gas mark 4. Line a rectangular tin, about 30 x 20 x 3 cm deep (12 x 8 x 1¼ in deep) with baking paper.

Beat the butter and sugar in a mixing bowl with a wooden spoon or electric whisk until pale and fluffy. Spoon in the maple syrup, then gradually add a little flour and egg alternately, beating well after each addition until combined.

Stir in the baking powder and mixed spice, pecans and the dates with their soaking liquid. Mix until thoroughly combined. Tip into the prepared tin, level with a spatula and bake for 45–50 minutes until a skewer inserted into the cake comes out clean. Lift the cake out of the tin and place on a cooling rack.

Wrap in foil to transport then cut into squares to serve.

Gingerbread People

MAKES: 25
Preparation time: 20 minutes
Cooking time: 10 minutes
Total time: 30 minutes

125 g (4½ oz) unsalted butter
100 g (3½ oz) dark muscovado sugar
4 tbsp golden syrup
325 g (11½ oz) plain flour, plus extra for dusting
1 tsp bicarbonate of soda
2 tsp ground ginger
Tubes of coloured writing icing (optional)

Pre-heat the oven to 170°C, gas mark 3. Line 2 baking trays with baking parchment. Melt the butter, sugar and golden syrup in a medium saucepan, stirring occasionally, then remove from the heat.

Sift the flour, bicarbonate of soda and ginger into a bowl and stir the melted ingredients into the dry ingredients to make a stiff dough.

Turn out the dough onto a lightly floured surface and roll to a thickness of about 5 mm (¼ in). Dip gingerbread people biscuit cutters into flour before cutting the dough. Place the gingerbread people onto the lined baking trays and bake, in batches, for 9–10 minutes until light golden brown.

Remove from the oven and leave to cool. When completely cool, decorate the gingerbread people with icing, if liked. The gingerbread biscuits can be stored in an airtight container for up to 2 weeks.

Cherry and Almond Tart

SERVES: 6
Preparation time: 15 minutes, plus chilling
Cooking time: 35 minutes
Total time: 50 minutes, plus chilling

50 g (2 oz) unsalted butter, melted, plus extra for greasing
Plain flour, for dusting
375 g (13 oz) ready-made sweet shortcrust pastry
1 medium egg, plus 1 medium egg yolk
100 g butter, softened
100 g (3½ oz) golden caster sugar, plus an extra 1 tbsp
100 g (3½ oz) ground almonds
1 tbsp Amaretto or brandy
300 g (10½ oz) cherries, halved and stoned
Crème fraîche or cream, to serve (optional)

Pre-heat the oven to 200°C, gas mark 6. Grease a 23 cm (9 in) diameter tart tin. Place a baking sheet in the oven to heat.

Roll out the pastry on a lightly floured surface slightly larger than the tin. Lift the pastry into the tin, pressing gently into the base and sides. Trim the edges and prick the base with a fork then chill for 20 minutes while you make the filling.

In a bowl, mix together the egg, egg yolk, butter, caster sugar, ground almonds and Amaretto or brandy. Spoon the mixture into the flan case.

Arrange the cherries on the almond paste. Sprinkle with the extra caster sugar and place on the pre-heated sheet. Bake for 30–35 minutes or until firm and light golden.

Leave to cool then cover with foil. Serve with a spoonful of crème fraîche or cream, if liked.

Pecan Banana Bread

MAKES: 10 SLICES
Preparation time: 15 minutes
Cooking time: 40 minutes
Total time: 55 minutes

100 g (3½ oz) butter, softened
175 g (6 oz) clear honey
2 eggs, beaten
2 large ripe bananas, roughly chopped
1/2 tsp ground mixed spice
225 g (8 oz) self-raising flour
100 g (3½ oz) pecan nuts, toasted and roughly chopped

Pre-heat the oven to 180°C, gas mark 4. Lightly grease a 1 kg (2 lb 4 oz) loaf tin and line the base and ends with a long strip of baking paper.

Place the butter, honey, eggs, bananas, mixed spice and flour in a food processor and blend until smooth. Alternatively, beat by hand with a wooden spoon. Add the pecans, and pulse or mix until just combined.

Pour the mixture into the prepared tin and level the top. Bake for 35–40 minutes until a skewer inserted into the centre of the loaf comes out clean, and the bread is golden and well risen. Allow the loaf to cool in the tin for 10 minutes then turn out. Remove the baking paper and leave to cool on a wire rack.

The loaf will keep for 4–5 days if stored in an airtight container. Keep in the container or wrap in foil to transport then serve sliced spread with butter, if liked.

Chocolate Hazelnut Cookies

MAKES: 18
Preparation time: 15 minutes
Cooking time: 12 minutes
Total time: 27 minutes

75 g (3 oz) butter, softened, plus extra for greasing
125 g (4½ oz) plain flour
½ tsp bicarbonate of soda
50 g (2 oz) light brown soft sugar
50 g (2 oz) caster sugar
1 tsp vanilla extract
1 large egg
50 g (2 oz) hazelnuts, chopped
100 g (3½ oz) plain chocolate, roughly chopped

Preheat the oven to 180°C, gas mark 4. Lightly grease 2 baking sheets.

Combine the butter, flour, bicarbonate of soda, light brown soft sugar, caster sugar and vanilla extract in a food processor and blend for a few seconds.

Add the egg, blend briefly, and then stir in the hazelnuts and chocolate.

Place 9 teaspoonfuls of cookie mixture on each baking sheet, making sure they are well spaced. Bake the cookies for 10–12 minutes until golden brown, and then leave them to cool on the baking sheets.

The cookies can be stored in an airtight container for 5 days.

Toffee Apple Flapjacks

MAKES: 18 SQUARES
Preparation time: 15 minutes
Cooking time: 35 minutes
Total time: 50 minutes

3 apples, such as Cox's, peeled, cored and cut into 2.5 cm
(1 in) pieces
Juice of ½ lemon
175 g (6 oz) unsalted butter
50 g (2 oz) light brown muscovado sugar
5 tbsp golden syrup
350 g (12 oz) porridge oats

Pre-heat the oven to 190°C, gas mark 5. Line an 18 x 28 cm (7 x 11 in) baking tin with baking paper. Place the apples and lemon juice in a small pan and bring to the boil. Cover and simmer for 5–7 minutes or until the apple is just soft. Use a fork to mash the apple to a soft purée and allow to cool slightly.

Place the butter, sugar and golden syrup in a pan and heat gently until the butter has melted. Remove from the heat and stir in the porridge oats until well combined.

Place half the mixture into the prepared tin and press down with the back of a spoon. Spread with the apple purée then cover with the remaining flapjack mixture.

Bake for 25 minutes or until golden brown. Remove from the oven, cut into 18 squares and allow to cool in the tin.

Remove the flapjacks from the tin and store in an airtight container for up to 2 days.

Drinks

Traditional Lemonade   Melon and Mint Crush

Winter Warmer   Spiced Cranberry and Apple Warmer

Rose Petal Bubbly

Traditional Lemonade

MAKES: 1 LITRE (1³/₄ PINTS)
Preparation time: 15 minutes, plus
cooling
Total time: 15 minutes, plus cooling

4 unwaxed lemons, washed
100 g (3½ oz) caster sugar, plus extra to taste

TO DECORATE (OPTIONAL):
Lemon slices
Mint leaves

Using a vegetable peeler, thinly peel the zest from the lemons, leaving as much white pith behind as possible. Squeeze the juice from the lemons. Place the zest, lemon juice and sugar in a large heatproof jug.

Pour in 600 ml (20 fl oz) boiling water and stir until the sugar has totally dissolved. Cover, and leave to cool completely.

Now, strain the lemon mixture into a serving jug with a lid, and discard the zest. Dilute with 400 ml (14 fl oz) chilled water and sweeten with extra sugar to taste. Serve decorated with lemon slices and mint leaves, if liked.

Melon and Mint Crush

SERVES: 8
Preparation time: 15 minutes, plus
chilling
Total time: 15 minutes, plus chilling

1 Galia melon, seeded and flesh scooped out
Handful mint leaves, stalks discarded and leaves finely
chopped
1–2 tbsp caster sugar, to taste

TO SERVE:
Vodka
Tonic water
Cucumber slices

Process the melon in a blender or food processor until smooth.

Stir the mint into the melon crush with 1–2 tablespoons caster
sugar, to taste. Pour the melon mixture into a plastic container,
seal well and chill.

Spoon 3–4 tablespoons melon crush and 1–2 tablespoons
vodka into each glass. Top up with tonic water, and stir. Add
slices of cucumber and serve. (For a non-alcoholic version, leave
out the vodka and top up with tonic, lemonade or sparkling
water.)

Winter Warmer

SERVES: 2

Preparation time: 5 minutes

Total time: 5 minutes

8 cloves

4 slices lemon

100 ml (3½ fl oz) whisky

4 tsp clear honey or golden syrup

3 tbsp lemon juice

Large pinch of ground cinnamon

200 ml (7 fl oz) hot water

Pour boiling water into a large flask to warm for 10–15 minutes. Discard the water.

Stick the cloves into the lemon skin. Put these and all the other ingredients into a jug and stir gently until the honey has dissolved.

Pour the drink into a flask for transporting.

This is a great drink for the winter point-to-points, though it's not for the drivers in the party – their alternative (which is also good for the children) is on the oppsoite page.

Spiced Cranberry and Apple Warmer

SERVES: 6
Preparation time: 5 minutes, plus
infusing
Cooking time: 5 minutes
Total time: 10 minutes, plus infusing

1 litre (1³/₄ pints) cranberry juice
250 ml (9 fl oz) fresh apple juice
2 cloves
1 cinnamon stick
Sugar, to taste
1 apple, halved, cored and thinly sliced

Place the cranberry and apple juice, cloves and cinnamon stick in a saucepan and warm gently – do not allow to boil.

Remove the pan from the heat and leave for 5 minutes, to allow the spices to infuse. Stir in sugar, to taste.

Pour boiling water into a large flask to warm for 10–15 minutes. Discard the water and pour the fruit warmer into the flask. Serve in mugs with slices of apple. (The drink can also be served cold.)

Rose Petal Bubbly

SERVES: 6
Preparation time: 3 minutes
Total time: 3 minutes

12 rose petals
1 egg white
4 tbsp caster suger
1 bottle Prosecco

Brush the rose petals all over with the egg white. Place the sugar in a plastic container that you can take to the picnic and add the rose petals, covering them with the sugar. Transport the rose petals to the picnic in this container to ensure the sugar stays stuck to them.

When ready to serve, place a few crystallised rose petals in the base of six glasses and top up with chilled Prosecco.

The rose petals never fail to cause a reaction. I like to use Prosecco rather than Champagne as I consider it sacrilege to doctor any decent Champagne!

Picnic Places

Dartmoor National Park   Brownsea Island   Jurassic Coast   Stonehenge and Avebury   Box Hill   White Cliffs of Dover   Longstock Park Water Garden   The Thames   The Windmill at Turville   A Day at the Races   Hay-on-Wye   Powis Castle and Gardens   A Day with Will in Shakespeare Country   Sherwood Forest and Robin Hood   Fountains Abbey and Studley Royal Water Garden   The Lake District   Lindisfarne   Floors Castle

Devon

DARTMOOR NATIONAL PARK

A strange and wonderful place, this National Park covers 953 square kilometres (368 square miles) in the middle of Devon. The source of the river Dart, which gave rise to its name this vast moorland has some of the bleakest as well as some of the most beautiful scenery anywhere in Britain. Mind you, it's not the place to get lost, as mists can come down without warning. I always make sure that I have a good map with hiking trails and walks marked on it.

This place of tors and cairns, rivers and ravines, as well as any number of prehistoric sights, really does have something for everyone. The girls always get very excited when they first see a Dartmoor pony, which of course means that we invariably visit the Miniature Pony Centre, near Moretonhampstead. This charming addition to any visit to Dartmoor is not just for children – we all enjoy being so close to the ponies and miniature donkeys as well as the pygmy goats. The centre provides a really good and interesting way to introduce children of all ages to these animals. And needless to say we also have to visit the Dartmoor Pony Heritage Trust because they do such good work in ensuring the survival of the ponies, particularly as their numbers are declining.

But it doesn't take us away from our real purpose, which is to see and explore the moor, and one

THE PICNIC

Vegetable and Feta Parcels

Smoked Mackerel and Bulghar Salad

Strawberry Bakewell Tart

The Picnic Site

At Dartmeet, where the east and west branches of the River Dart meet – lovely meadows, beautiful countryside and close to the miniature farm, where we can donate all our leftovers!

of our favourite occupations is visiting the various 'letterboxes' throughout the expanse and signing the books we find there. (Letterboxing is a tradition that began with early walkers where they would leave their calling cards and a stamped addressed envelope in boxes hidden in tree roots and under rocks, for the next 'explorer' to come across and resend. Now it is much more organised, with books to sign and information to be passed on from one traveller to another.)

While this area is stunningly beautiful on a brilliant summer's day, you begin to appreciate the real atmosphere of the place when you see the clouds darkening on the horizon. This really does help you to understand why Dartmoor has been the source of such myths and legends as the headless horsemen, the strange black dog, not to mention the innumerable ghost stories and the wilful pixies! It is easy to understand how it has inspired writers such as Agatha Christie and Sir Arthur Conan Doyle.

But more than anything we all enjoy learning something new about nature, whether it's wild flowers, butterflies or birds and occasionally the girls make lists and draw pictures as we go, so that we do not forget all we have seen. I am particularly keen on Grimspound, that amazing Bronze Age settlement with its burial mounds and hut circles.

CHEAT'S PICNIC
- **The Royal Oak Inn, Dunsford** – serves locally produced food and cider.
- **Farrants Farm, Dunsford** – for cider, cider vinegar, honey, mustard and jams.
- **Curworthy Cheese, Stockbeare Farm, near Okehampton** – for local cheese.
- **Higher Murchington Farm, Chagford** – for Devonshire Farmhouse Ice Cream and clotted cream.
- **Bramble Torre, Dittisham, near Dartmouth** – farm shop and pick-your-own salads and wonderful herbs.

ALSO IN THE AREA
- **Buckland Abbey, Yelverton** – 700 years of history have hidden in these buildings which were once the home of Sir Francis Drake.
- **Finch Foundry** – a water-powered forge still in good working order almost 200 years after it was built, with some fun demonstrations.
- **Castle Drogo, near Exeter** – an Edwin Lutyens' masterpiece, dubbed 'the last castle to be built in England'.
- **Brimblecombe's Cider, Farrants Farm, Dunsford** – see how cider has been brewed in these parts for over 450 years.
- **Lydford Gorge, near Okehampton** – spectacular river gorge and waterfall. Not for the faint-hearted!

Devon and Dorset
JURASSIC COAST

THE PICNIC

Mediterranean
Picnic Bread

Simple Crab Pâté

Gingerbread people

We are rather keen on dinosaurs in our house, and one of our all-time favourite outings is to the Natural History Museum in London, which is surprising for me as I was left there on a school trip at the age of 10. An interesting reflection on that era is that my parents blamed me for being left behind – not the teachers! So it is even more fun to visit the Jurassic Coast which runs for more than 145 kilometres (90 miles) from Dorset through to East Devon and is as dramatic as any coastal area you can find anywhere in the world. Of course we haven't explored every part of it – that will take many years of outings and picnics – but it provides one of our favourite days out as it

has seaside and countryside with lots to do and lots to learn. No matter how often we go, we always find something exciting and fossil hunting in our family has become very competitive.

The Jurassic Coast was the UK's first natural World Heritage Site. One of our favourite parts is in and around Lyme Regis. We all love the town, the walks along the coast and fossil hunting on the beach, and, if the weather should suddenly turn for the worse, we can head for the Aquarium or the Philpot Museum, which has a terrific collection of fossils. In fact, the museum is in the former home of one the best palaeontologists England has produced, Mary Anning, who has become a real heroine for the girls. My mother-in-law comes from this part of the country and we often pop in on the way to Lyme Regis to get the girls in the mood for dinosaurs! My wife Judith, our cultural expert, reminds us that *The French Lieutenant's Woman* was filmed in Lyme Regis and that Jane Austen's novel *Persuasion* is partly set in the area.

The coast is truly exciting as it chronicles some 185 million years of the earth's history, taking in the Triassic, Jurassic and Cretaceous ages (we have spelling contests on the journey down!). I always make sure that we have a fossil guide and a small magnifying glass, while of course no picnic is complete without a pair of binoculars. The last time we were there I met somebody who had seen bottle-nose dolphins the day before… we are still hoping.

Because Lyme Regis is so pretty and popular we tend not to go in the height of summer, and I always leave the car in one of the designated car parks. I might drive down to the harbour and unload the picnic there

(my useful tip is to keep everything light) and go back to park. We mostly head off west and find somewhere to make a base. We like the beach because you can find a sheltered spot in the undercliffs, where we leave our stuff while we go for a walk, a paddle or a swim before we begin our fossil hunt. However, we always end our day with a brisk cliff walk and then come back to the Cobb where we reward ourselves with an ice cream.

The Cobb is one of the most famous landmarks of the town. It's been there since the 13th century to provide a breakwater for protection as well as an artificial harbour. It has, of course, been destroyed a number of times by storms and sea, but it has always been rebuilt. In fact, this coastline is notorious for its landslides which is why it is such a rich hunting ground for ammonites and other fossils.

The Picnic Site

Stay on the coast and look for a sheltered spot at either picturesque Charmouth Beach near Lyme Regis (it's close to Charmouth Heritage Coast Centre in case the weather turns) or Swanage Bay, near Old Harry Rocks and Ballard Down, for great scenery.

CHEAT'S PICNIC

● The George at Charmouth serves local foods and ales, while the Pilot Boat Inn in Bridge Street, Lyme Regis has fresh local fish and seafood, and the Jurassic Seafood Wine Bar supports local producers.
● Otherwise hunt out farmers' markets and Womens' Institute markets, as well as heading for: Long Crichel Bakery, near Wimborne – for bread and cakes; Becklands Farm, near Bridport – a good place for meat, vegetables (to bring home) and fruit, as well as terrific lemon curd; Woolsery Cheese, on the way to Dorchester – for a serious selection of home-produced soft cheeses, as well as their own Cheddar.

ALSO IN THE AREA

● **Portland Island** – where the stone comes from. The most famous building stone we have, used by Sir Christopher Wren and in many of the UK's grandest houses as well as in the building of Westminster Abbey.
● **RSPB Bird Reserve at Radipole Lake** – great for twitchers of all ages.
● **Black Ven Landslide** – National Trust site which, due to massive changes over the last 50 years, is great for fossil hunting.
● **Corfe Castle** – 1,000 years old, and currently with extensive restoration work in progress so access restricted in some places. However, it is still wild and wonderful.

● **Kingston Lacey** – beautiful house and gardens, impressive art collection and location of Badbury Rings, an Iron Age fort (Badbury Rings also hosts point-to-point racing three or four times throughout the year – have a picnic there: see page 168).
● **Castle Drogo** – last castle to be built in England, designed by Sir Edwin Lutyens, and has the highest National Trust Garden.
● **Studland Beach and Nature Reserve** – almost five kilometres (three miles) of fantastic sandy beach which is also home to rare birds.

Poole, Dorset

BROWNSEA ISLAND

This is the largest of the eight islands in Poole harbour. It is owned by the National Trust, and open from March until the end of October. For such a small place, it has an enormous amount to offer. The girls are particularly taken with it, as it is one of the few places in this country where you can still see red squirrels. Even though it is home to them, they are such shy and secretive creatures that it is still quite difficult to spot them, which is why finding them makes any visit so much more exciting.

Brownsea has an extraordinary number of different landscapes and terrain – coastal, lagoon, woodland, heathland and freshwater lakes – making it an important wildlife location. As well as the squirrels, it also has deer (including Sika deer) and peacocks, and during the winter is home to large flocks of birds, including egrets and avocets.

The first mention of the island dates back to the 7th century when a hermit living there used light beacons to guide boats into harbour, an act that wasn't wasted on Henry VIII who recognised its strategic importance and fortified the harbour with a castle. The castle is now leased and used as a holiday home for employees of the John Lewis Partnership.

Throughout the centuries the island has been owned by a number of different families who have improved the quay, the castle and harbour, built a church, and planted a wide variety of trees and shrubs. It is now most famous for being the home of scouting and guiding as Robert Baden-Powell held the first scout camp here in 1907.

THE PICNIC

Seafood Pan-bagnat

Roasted Vegetable Salad

Chocolate, Walnut and Date Brownies

The Picnic Site

Either Church Field in the south-east corner of the island with views over the lagoon, castle and church, or Penelope Park in the centre of the island where you can lunch under pine trees and admire the peacocks, or any stretch of beach.

I like taking the ferry across from Poole (it departs twice an hour) and the trip takes just 15 minutes. For first-time visitors it is worth noting that there are free guided tours, or there are a number of leaflets with easy-to-follow walks and rambles. We normally take one of these, and the one thing we all want to see is a red squirrel – such a pity these are now almost extinct in southern England. And of course we always promise ourselves that one year we will come back to see a performance at the Open Air Theatre, which is usually held mid to late August, and is always Shakespeare.

I must say I like early summer here and if the sun is shining, there surely isn't a more appealing view than the one across to the harbour. No wonder George IV was so taken with the place when he visited in 1818 – 'I had no idea I had such a delightful spot in my kingdom' – was his reaction.

CHEAT'S PICNIC
● **Visit the tea-room on the quay at Brownsea Island.**

ALSO IN THE AREA

● **Corfe Castle, Wareham** – a majestic ruin, over 1,000 years old, rising above the Isle of Purbeck.

● **Clouds Hill, Wareham** – the tiny cottage that was once the rural retreat of T.E. Lawrence, otherwise known as Lawrence of Arabia, which has an exhibition of his life.

● **Hardy's Cottage, near Dorchester** – the birthplace of Wessex's famous novelist and where he lived as a young adult. Wonderful cottage garden.

● **Studland Beach and Nature Reserve** – glorious sandy beach and wildlife haven.

● **Athelhampton House, Dorchester** – one of the finest 15th-century houses in England. Great grounds, with topiary pyramids in the walled garden and a terrific Tudor trail for children.

● **Cerne Abbas Giant** – otherwise known as the Rude Giant, a huge outline carved into the chalk hillside which can be seen for kilometres, although the best viewpoint is from the A352. He was disguised during the Second World War so that enemy planes couldn't use him as a landmark.

Wiltshire
STONEHENGE AND AVEBURY

I've always been fascinated by these two strange, mysterious and magical sites and really enjoy taking the girls there because there is always something new to discover. It is extraordinary but every time I visit I really do see something different – it may be because it is a different season or a different time of day, but these monuments are compelling.

THE PICNIC

Chinese Chicken Drumsticks

Couscous Salad with Roasted Vegetables

Cherry and Almond Tart

Now that the girls are getting older they are beginning to share my enthusiasm, although it is difficult for any of us to comprehend just how

these circles came about some 3,500 years ago. And Lily still wonders why the dinosaurs didn't knock them over. Yes, we know the stones made a journey of over 320 kilometres (200 miles), but how? We know that the entire construction of Stonehenge took over 1,500 years and was in three phases, but we don't know why. And most important of all, we don't really know why it was constructed, in spite of the many theories from astronomical purposes to a place of sacrifice and worship (although we do know that a large number of charred human remains have been found in the area). I have never visited during the solstices, but I plan to do so when the girls are much older – it must be quite wonderful and awe-inspiring.

What makes these places so magical is that they are some of the earliest examples of Britain's ancient culture and it's humbling to stand close to one of those vast stones and attempt to understand what exactly was going on. And although I would like to get closer and closer, I am delighted that both English Heritage and the National Trust look after these sites so carefully to preserve them for a few more millennia. When I first visited Stonehenge as a boy, you could walk around without impunity or restriction, but now a fence keeps visitors at a distance, which, given the number of tourist today, is essential to minimise destruction at the site.

We always start off by calling in at the Visitors' Centre to see if there have been any new findings or discoveries before visiting the site of Stonehenge itself, although the great exciting moment is when we first spot it from the road. When we have had our moments of

wonder, we head off to Avebury – how extraordinary it is that these two monumental prehistoric sites should be a mere 40 kilometres (25 miles apart).

One of the most important Neolithic monuments in Europe, Avebury is a favourite place of mine – I love walking around it, I love the sense of mystery which surrounds it and I love its museum and the stories of Alexander Keiller, who made his money from Dundee marmalade and spent much of it helping conserve Avebury and its surrounds, including re-erecting some of the fallen and buried stones. It's a great place for walks too, so often after our picnic we try to get a good walk – I particularly like taking the path across the fields to Silbury Hill, while one day I have promised myself I will walk the Ridgeway.

The Picnic Site

At Stonehenge it's easy to find a spot in the fields around the site with a good view of the stones, while at Avebury you can enjoy your picnic amongst the stones and earthworks, but do remember to treat the place with the respect it deserves.

CHEAT'S PICNIC

● Head for either Warminster or Salisbury farmers' markets where you can find:ame and venison pies and sausages (some for now, some for home) at GM Country Sports & Game (bison and elk products too); Mill House Country Kitchens for freshly baked bread and cakes.
● Rosemary's Preserves, Highgate Farm, Wootton Bassett – worth a detour for jams.
● The pub at Longleat – serves good local food but can be pricy.

ALSO IN THE AREA

● **Silbury Hill, West Kennet** – this is the largest prehistoric man-made mound in Europe. Access may be restricted due to conservation, but it's still a wonder worth seeing.
● **Lacock Abbey and the Fox Talbot Museum of Photography, near Chippenham** – a wonderful fusion of thirteenth-century nunnery and nineteenth-century photographic experiments.
● **Old Wardour Castle, Tisbury** – a truly photogenic fourteenth-century hexagonal tower house – grand and impressive.
● **Stourhead, Stourton** – one of the grandest of stately homes stunning gardens and parkland in the country, with wonderful walks, follies and gazebos.

● **Great Chalfield Manor and Garden, near Melksham** – a charming fifteenth-century manor house with a great Arts and Crafts-style garden.
● **Dyrham Park, near Bath** – a spectacular William-and-Mary house with landscaped gardens and an extensive deer park.
● **Longleat, Warminster** – one of the most famous stately homes and one of the first to open to the public. It began life as an Augustinian priory, then became a family home before becoming a safari park. It also has a narrow-gauge railway, butterfly garden and pets' corner.

Tadworth, Surrey
BOX HILL

THE PICNIC

Prosciutto, Porcini and Olive Schiacciata

Pasta and Broccoli Salad with Watercress Pesto

Spanish Almond Torte with Lemon Syrup

One of the joys of this country is that we are never very far from woodland, open space and fresh air – and Box Hill in Surrey is a supreme example of this. One minute you are toddling through suburbia on the outskirts of London, and the next you can be enjoying the wide open spaces and physical freedom of this fantastic area of 1,200 acres.

Given to the nation in 1914 by philanthropist Leopold Salomons of nearby Norbury Park, it has been managed and looked after by the National Trust as well as being extended by trusts and donations. A refreshing and regenerating playground for those who live in the nearby towns and cities, it is a constantly changing backdrop for those seeking nature and fresh air. See it in spring when the buds and blossoms decorate the trees, in the height of summer with its abundance of birds and other wildlife as well as luxuriant wildflowers, including a dozen or so species of wild orchids. The beech,

The Picnic Site
The new shaded picnic area, which also has seats, near the summit of the hill – great views.

CHEAT'S PICNIC
● **There are lots of farmers' markets in the immediate vicinity (Wallington, Epsom, Dorking and Guildford), offering everything from honey to home-made cakes, as well as cheeses and organic drinks. Also call in at:**
● **Cranleigh Organic Farm Shop – for good cheese, salads and vegetables.**
● **Applegarth Farm Shop, Grayshott – for vegetables, bread and eggs.**
● **Headley Stores, near Epsom – deli for meats, pâtés, cheeses and breads.**

oak and elm which cover Box Hill's slopes and walks provide a blaze of red and gold in autumn, while winter has its own special beauty – stark and still and, when covered in frost, it is a completely magical experience. Best of all there are walks and trails for every age and level of fitness – with short strolls, long walks, hiking trails, nature trails and ones specially designed for families.

The beauty of Box Hill has reached a much wider audience – both nationally and internationally – since it became the setting for a pivotal scene in Jane Austen's *Emma*, when the interfering but well-meaning heroine set out to discover 'what everybody found so much worth seeing'. Our cultural adviser, Judith, tries to persuade us to watch the DVD of *Emma* before we go, just to put it in context for us, but secretly I think she is so fond of the book and the film she just wants to see it again herself!

ALSO IN THE AREA
● **Leith Hill, near Dorking** – the highest point in south-east England, with panoramic views from its gothic tower and great walks on the heath.
● **Polesden Lacey, Great Bookham** – a grand Edwardian house with opulent interiors.
● **Claremont Landscape Garden, Esher** – wonderfully English landscaped garden with lake (and 52 species of water-fowl), ha-ha, grotto and amphitheatre.
● **Clandon Park, near Guildford** – a Palladian mansion with a magnificent white marble hall.
● **Hatchlands Park, near Guildford** – 18th-century house with Robert Adam interiors, Gertrude Jekyll garden and glorious bluebell wood.

Dover, Kent
WHITE CLIFFS OF DOVER

We still like travelling to the continent by boat – the voyage seems to put us all in the holiday mood. And so we often see one of the most famous of all our natural landmarks and easily the most symbolic – before there was air travel and the Channel Tunnel, the white cliffs of Dover were both the first thing travellers saw on coming to the UK, and the last thing they saw when leaving.

This pure white chalkland was part of the landmass long before Britain was an island, another reason why it is so potent an emblem. Added to which it's a great place to walk and enjoy fresh sea air, not to mention its spectacular views across the Channel and the chance to observe one of the world's busiest shipping lanes.

The best place to start is at the visitors' centre – the Gateway to the White Cliffs – which has truly informative and imaginative displays of some eight kilometres (five miles) of coastline, explaining its geological strata as well as the flora and fauna which can be found there. Historically, of course, the cliffs have great importance as the last bastions before an invasion, but further east along the coast the South Foreland lighthouse provides its own history lesson. South Foreland was used by Faraday as the first example of an electrically lit lighthouse, while Marconi used it for the first

THE PICNIC

Hot-smoked Trout and Leek Frittata

Parmesan Twists

Apricot Sponge with Walnuts

international radio broadcast to France. This is yet another place where we go into twitcher mode, trying to spot all the seabirds that flock to the area – we are getting very good on the kittiwakes, but then we should as there are supposed to be some 1,100 or more mating couples in what is believed to be the best nesting site in Kent – we have occasionally spotted a Peregrine falcon. Inevitably it turns into a game of who can count the most! This is yet another reason why it is a good idea to have a pair of binoculars with you on picnic outings, and more than ever here, when you can spot the French coast on clear days.

CHEAT'S PICNIC

Dover Farmers' Market has a comprehensive and changing group of farm shops from the Garden of England – good cheese, great apples and very good wine.

ALSO IN THE AREA

- **Dover Castle** – often called the 'Key to England' and it has a warren of secret wartime tunnels.
- **Walmer Castle and Gardens** – the castle is part of a chain of defence against a Catholic invasion from Europe, built during Henry VIII's reign, while the gardens are extensive, including the newest addition specially designed for the Queen Mother's 95th birthday.
- **The Western Heights** – one of the most impressive fortifications against a French invasion, begun during the Napoleonic Wars.
- **Deal Castle** – another magnificent Tudor coastal fort.
- **South Foreland Lighthouse** – a distinctive Victorian lighthouse.

Stockbridge, Hampshire
LONGSTOCK PARK WATER GARDEN

As a family we enjoy gardens. We love reading about them, watching TV programmes about them and tending and caring for our own garden – and, of course, we love visiting them, whether they be wild, formal, children's playgrounds, historical or specialist. One of our favourites is Longstock Park Water Garden, and each time we visit I remind myself how fortunate I am to be associated with a company which has both a desire and a duty to own and preserve such elements of English tradition and heritage. Waitrose is part of the John Lewis Partnership, which owns and manages what has been voted the finest water garden in the world, and it is open to the public on the first and third Sundays of each month throughout the summer, with all proceeds going to local charities (although the third Sunday in June is invariably reserved for the National Garden Scheme).

No matter when you visit, it is always a joy to spot not just the different flowers, shrubs and grasses, but the amazing plethora of birds, insects and butterflies. The girls are particularly keen on these and we always take a picture chart as a guide and mark how many we can spot, along with dragonflies and water boatmen.

The garden, almost seven acres of it, was constructed mainly in the early part of the 20th century, using water diverted from the River Test to make the lakes and connecting canals – and it is these water features which make this habitat so extraordinary. Just by sitting still and watching the water carefully you can spot any number of freshwater fish such as pike and bream, as well a number of different Japanese Koi carp, all hungry for bread. Then there are the birds – the kingfishers alone are worth a visit, while the place is bejewelled with woodpeckers (three different species), herons, moorhens, larks and many more.

Of course, what we all love are the plants and as we go around we make notes of the ones we hope we will see on sale in the nursery at the end. The water lilies are what the place is famed for, and depending which report you read, there are between 40 and 80 different types. The girls, when not running around, love drawing them as they are such a perfect shape.

We spend rather a long time, and often much money, in the nursery, which is situated in the old walled kitchen garden. Apart from housing the National Collections of Buddleias and Clematis Viticella, it also has the most stunning 100-year-old herbaceous border which is the envy of everyone who sees it. The great thing about the nursery is that you can order in advance for different season and I often have to be restrained from ordering beautiful, but inappropriate plants for my own garden.

The other element of Longstock which pleases me greatly is that it is part of the Leckford Estate – home to the Waitrose farm. The farm supplies some of our stores as well as having its own shop. We always make a point of visiting for treats to take home.

THE PICNIC

Poached Salmon with Watercress

Make Yourself Pasta Salad

Chocolate Hazelnut Cookies

The Picnic Site
Anywhere you can lay a blanket in this beautiful area.

CHEAT'S PICNIC

● **Try to coincide with Winchester Farmers' Market and find: goats' cheese from Rosary Goats' Cheese, and other types from Lyburn Farmhouse Cheesemakers; fudge from Candy Carnival; fruit and salads from Durleighmarsh Farm Shop.**

● **The Restaurant at Netley Abbey offers more substantial meals, also using locally produced ingredients.**

● **The Mayfly pub on the River Test, near Stockbridge.**

● **The Peat Spade Inn in Longstock Village.**

ALSO IN THE AREA

● **Netley Abbey** – the most complete Cistercian Abbey in the south of England which was visited often by Jane Austen and painted by Constable, while the nearby Royal Victoria Hospital was supposedly where Dr. Watson of Sherlock Holmes-fame trained.

● **Wolvesey Castle** – a 12th-century Norman keep which became the chief residence of the Bishops of Winchester.

● **The Vyne at Sherborne St. John** – a wonderful 16th-century house which has been in the same family for over 350 years and boasts a lovely Tudor chapel and great gardens and woodland.

● **Hinton Ampner** – another wonderful garden with magnificent topiary, and gardeners on hand to answer your questions.

● **The Test Valley** – the Test is one of the finest fly-fishing waters in the country and exploring its banks or simply sitting on them to enjoy them is a glorious thing to do on a summer afternoon.

● **Stockbridge** – lots of interesting independent shops. Feed the fish!

Pangbourne, Berkshire
THE THAMES

For many of us, this part of the River Thames will be forever associated with Mole, Ratty and Toad. The location of the book *The Wind in the Willows* is never identified as such, but once you know that author Kenneth Grahame lived in the village, and once you have experienced a stroll along part of the National Thames Pathway on a sunny day and looked out across the water meadows, you feel in your heart this must have been his inspiration. It is such a quintessential English scene, and so wonderfully described in the book, that even a first-time visitor feels he already knows it.

Of course we get ourselves in the mood for such an outing by reading extracts from the adventures, and we have a recording that we play in the car on the way there. And it's a strange sensation but Judith and I still get the same sense of fun and wonderment from the words as the girls do. It's a book that will never go out of fashion, and will always appeal to those of us who get great enjoyment from the whole concept of messing about on the river. But Kenneth Grahame didn't have that part of the river all to

THE PICNIC

Bacon and Pea Quiche

Traditional Lemonade

Eton Mess

The Picnic Site
Best places are either in the meadows or at Beale Park – head for some shade and enjoy.

himself, for Jerome K. Jerome mentions the local pub – the Swan Public House – in his wonderful comedy *Three Men in a Boat*.

We tend to hire an electric launch from the Swan Hotel in Streatley. Heading down the river we like to visit Beale Park, particularly to see the goats and the ponies, and there is much excitement if we spot a kingfisher among the many other birds in the park! As we sail down to Pangbourne the water meadows there are the perfect destination for a summer outing. Or heading up the river our only task is to find an ideal spot for a picnic, and often we are spoilt for choice. And before we go home, a walk through the village is always a must.

ALSO IN THE AREA

● **Basildon Park, near Reading** – as famous for its shell room as for being one of the locations in the filming of *Pride and Prejudice*.

● **Ashdown House, near Lambourn** – 17th-century Dutch-style house with an Iron Age hill fort in the grounds.

● **Greys Court, Henley-on-Thames** – Tudor manor with beautiful rose gardens, a wisteria walk and a maze.

● **Fawley Court, Henley-on-Thames** – wonderful house designed by Sir Christopher Wren and with a Grinling Gibbons carved ceiling in the drawing room.

● **Wellington Country Park, near Reading** – part of the Duke of Wellington's estate. Good nature trails and wildlife.

Buckinghamshire
THE WINDMILL AT TURVILLE

Cobstone Mill at Ibstone, near Turville, is more than just an historic building – for centuries it was a hard-working mill and then it turned into a movie star. The current building was constructed in 1816, although on the site of a much older one, and received international stardom for its appearances in the film *Chitty Chitty Bang Bang*.

A proper working mill, its last job was to grind cereal throughout World War One, after which it fell into disrepair until spotted by a talent scout for the film. Although it was cosmetically restored for the movie, it wasn't until it was subsequently bought by actress Hayley Mills and her first husband Roy Boulting that the mill and its accompanying cottage were totally restored. Since then, it has made a number of appearances in both TV programmes and films, which is not surprising, since its setting is charming and

THE PICNIC

Spinach, Parmesan and Spaghetti Frittata

Pizzettes

Blueberry Coconut Muffins

quintessentially British, as it sits right on top of the ridge with great views across the Buckinghamshire countryside down to the vale of Hambleden.

If you are all feeling particularly energetic, my tip is to park in the village and walk to the top of the ridge with your picnic – it's easy to find a sunny spot in the field next to the windmill. However, for slowcoaches or the slightly idle, park in the lane nearby and walk the last few hundred yards – it's all on the flat! If you choose this option, you may want a good walk across the ridge to help digest the picnic goodies or when the breeze is right, fly kites. We play the *Chitty Chitty Bang Bang* CD in the car on the way to Turville to get into the mood (having watched the DVD the day before) and sing along on the walk, *Truly Scrumptious*, *Toot Sweets* and *Chitty Chitty Bang Bang* being the favourites. Not too loudly, though – we don't want to frighten the animals or other walkers.

Turville itself is a very pretty village – it is even mentioned in the Anglo-Saxon chronicle in 796 as Thyrefeld (which means 'dry field'), while the manor of Turville once belonged to St Albans' abbey but was seized by the crown in the Dissolution of the Monasteries in 1547. The manor house has been rebuilt as Turville Manor and is currently the home of Lord Sainsbury (of Sainsbury's supermarket family). And while you're walking and admiring the building, it will strike you that so much of it seems familiar – and it is. Here are just a few of its film and TV credits:
● *Went the Day Well* – a 1942 war movie in which it was the village invaded by German paratroopers
● *The Vicar of Dibley* – many of the outdoor scenes
● *Little Britain* – the Dafydd Thomas scene
● *Midsomer Murders*
● *Miss Marple*

The Picnic Site
The field by the side of the windmill (see opposite).

CHEAT'S PICNIC
Head for West Wycombe to the Plant and Harvest farm shop and café and select from what is in season.

ALSO IN THE AREA
● **The Manor House, Hambleden** – birthplace of Lord Cardigan – he of the Light Brigade.
● **Bletchley Park, Milton Keynes** – famous for the encryption machine and its huge range of Churchill memorabilia. Also there is the well-known Home of Rest for Horses in nearby Speen.
● **National Trust village of West Wycombe** – has Britain's oldest garden centre and farm shop, Plant and Harvest. If you have time, visit the nearby Hell-Fire Caves and Sir Edward Dashwood's Country Home and Estate – an extraordinary garden and architectural folly.

Andoversford, Gloucestershire
A Day at the Races

I have always had a strong affinity for the countryside and its importance not only to our culture and heritage, but also to our future. And I have tried to share this at all times with my daughters, who so far, fortunately, seem as passionate about it as me. One of the many ways the countryside and the people who work there share their lives and customs with us is at point-to-point races. While we all might like the smart outings at the fashionable courses like Ascot and Goodwood, the real heart of horse-racing can be experienced at a point-to-point race meeting. It's a terrific gathering ground for everyone who lives and works in the area – breeders, farmers and producers all having the most tremendous fun, often in spite of the weather. Many meetings take place during the winter months, so all you do is make sure you dress warmly, especially when it comes to boots and hats, and have the right, warming food.

We love these events, and often arrange to meet friends at them. You should see us – cars parked next to each other, boots open, children exploring the stalls, paddock and horseboxes, and we adults preparing barbecues, making coffee and tea, and having a quick nip of sloe gin (not the drivers, of course!) while organising the picnic. We even have one friend who has a device which helps bring the red wine to room temperature via the car's cigarette lighter!

A point-to-point is the venue for a totally different type of picnic – warming soups, chilli con carne in a wide-lipped flask, baked potatoes kept hot in layers of newspaper and that wonderful smell of sausages and chops grilling in the open air. This is where good, traditional English food comes into its own, too – filling Cornish pasties, great chunks of cheese with pickle, apple turnovers and the best fruitcake.

THE PICNIC

Italian Bean and Vegetable Soup

Barbecued Sausages with Fresh Mango Chutney

Winter Warmer

The Picnic Site

As close to the rails as you can get and best of all between jumps two and three. Don't forget waterproofs, because even if the weather's good, there is a chance the grass will be damp.

Point-to-points take place all over the country and we like to choose a different one every time. I invariably trawl through the programme until I find one which has a really close relationship with the local farming community. We need farmers and I wholeheartedly believe in fully supporting them, which is why the Cotswold Vale Farmers' point-to-point at Andoversford, just outside Cheltenham, is one of our favourites. Indeed, anywhere in the Cotswolds is a real treat for a day out. Not only does it have some of the prettiest honey-coloured stone villages and towns, but also gently rolling countryside and some of the most wonderful stately homes and gardens.

Cheltenham itself is worth finding time to visit before the racing starts. It's a near-perfect Regency town which we have all seen countless times on our TV screens, as many of its streets, crescents and buildings have had starring roles in any number of costume dramas from *Vanity Fair* to *The House of Eliott*. But it is the relationship with the countryside, and in Gloucestershire's case as a producer of some great traditional foods, that attracts us back.

PS: Another good day at the races is at Cartmel, mid-way between Morecambe Bay and Lake Windermere, which we love both for the great day out and because it is home to one of our favourite foods – sticky toffee pudding!

CHEAT'S PICNIC

● With over 50 stalls, nearby **Stroud Farmers' Market** has won the prize for best market for the second year running. Look here for The Handmade Scotch Egg Company; Simon Weaver's Soft Cheese Company – delicious Cotswold Organic Blue and Cotswold Organic Brie.
● Trout pâté and smoked trout from Cockleford Trout Farm.
● Hayles Fruit Farm offers great apple juice and terrific Badger's Bottom Cider.
● The Royal Oak, Prestbury – serves locally produced food plus a selection of real ales and ciders.

ALSO IN THE AREA

● **The town of Cheltenham itself** – The Pump Room is particularly worth a visit.
● **Sherborne** – a short drive away on the Dorset border, with its glorious abbey and two castles, one of which was built by Sir Walter Raleigh.
● **Lodge Park and Sherborne Estate** – built by a 17th-century gambler and hunchback, it has a fantastic deer park and a grandstand.
● **Prinknash Abbey** – nine centuries old, this Benedictine abbey is renowned for its pottery as well as the manufacturing of incense (a must to take home).

Hay-on-Wye, Herefordshire
THE TOWN OF BOOKS

Running along the River Wye, Hay is right on the border between England and Wales, straddling both. It's a tiny but perfect market town and we enjoy going there simply because, for somewhere so small, there is so much to see. Apart from being situated in the Brecon Beacons National Park and within striking distance of the Black Mountains – two of the most beautiful areas in the UK – it has two castles, albeit ruined, and best of all some 30 second-hand bookshops, which is the reason it is now known worldwide as the 'town of books'.

I love bookshops of all types and it is really difficult to get me away from one once I'm ensconced. Sometimes on a visit to Hay, I find myself hoping for rain just to give me the perfect excuse to linger in as many as I want.

However, Judith and the girls now limit the amount of time I am allowed to spend inside. You never know what you might find in one of these establishments, and an hour is never going to be enough, especially when you think that in the shop owned by Richard Booth, the self-styled 'King of Hay', there are more than 400,000 books.

We always start at Rose's Books, which has the best collection of children's books, many of which are out of print and some of which are extremely rare. And while the girls are nosing about here, I set off on my own little adventure. (You can find out where all the bookshops are, as well as who specialises in what, from the free town guide which you can pick up in any of the shops.) There are a couple of great travel and map shops that I could spend weeks in. However, once my hour is up, we have to move on.

The town itself, with its little cobbled streets, picturesque houses and the castles, is always worth spending some time in. Now that the girls are older, I think the next time we visit we will hire a couple of canoes for an excursion on the river – we might even find

THE PICNIC

Goats' Cheese
and Pesto Tart

Sausage Rolls with
Cranberries and Sage

Cranberry Rock Buns

The Picnic Site
Head for the Riverside Walk (adjacent to St Mary's Church) which is part of the Brecon Beacons park system and is well signposted. It follows the old railway line alongside the banks of the Wye. An ideal spot for a picnic.

another picnic spot. However, a walk along the river bank is a must for any visitor, for the scenery is outstanding and the view across to the Black Mountains just makes me wish I could sketch or paint. Late summer is a good time to visit, as everything looks golden and warm, and while it attracts visitors throughout the year, the one time to avoid is during the Hay Festival when, for about 10 days in late May/early June, it becomes the centre of the book world. For a tiny little town on the borders of two small countries, it really does attract the biggest names in the literary world, and when the girls are older, we have promised to visit one year.

CHEAT'S PICNIC

● If it's raining, Hay is awash with good cafés and pubs serving local foods, ciders and beers. There are also good farmers' markets at Leominster and Ross-on-Wye, as well as local Women's Institute markets.
● Producers to look out for include: The Dairy House at Weobley; Berrow Honey; The Handmade Scotch Egg Company; Love Patisserie (you can visit at Gardeners Cottage, Clifford)
● I always make an effort to look for New Shepherd's Ice Cream, and if we can't find anyone selling it on the day, will make a detour through Hereford to its shop. It's made from sheep's milk and is delicious.

ALSO IN THE AREA

● **The Brecon Beacons National Park** – a place not just of great beauty but of great wonder too. Just head down Forest Road to the Information Centre and see what there is to discover. Guided walks are often on offer and there is an impressive programme of children's activities.
● **Hay Castle** – a mixture of thirteenth-century fortification and a Jacobean manor. Of course it has a bookshop too.

● **Brecon Castle** – an 11th-century fortification in a great spot overlooking the River Usk.
● **Dore Abbey** – formerly a Cistercian monastery and now maintained by the Church of England, just 20 minutes from Hay.
● **Tretower Castle and Court** – a fourteenth-century mixture of a military fortification and what must have been a rather grand manor house. Only about 30 minutes south of Hay, it is worth the detour.

Welshpool, Powys

Powis Castle and Gardens

How do you get two whales in a mini? Go along the M5 and turn left! The magnificent Powis Castle is a real treat. It has been the home of the same family for almost 400 years, and boasts wonderful Italianate gardens and an extraordinary collection of Indian memorabilia dating from the time the Herbert family married into the Clive family, and had access to Robert Clive's Indian heritage. There is so much to see here – Gainsboroughs in the drawing room, maharajahs' treasures in the museum and plants for sale...

Overlooking the Severn valley, this medieval fortress sits high above the town, master of all it surveys. Its 17th-century terraced garden is the nearest thing to an Italian renaissance garden in the UK, and add to that a woodland wilderness, beautifully designed parkland, a kitchen garden, flower garden, some of the finest clipped yews anywhere, an orangery, terraces, fountains and a great collection of statuary and sculpture.

We are never quite sure where to begin – house or garden – because there is always something we want to remind ourselves of, or

THE PICNIC

Leek and Cheddar tart

Broad Bean, Ham and Feta Salad

Raspberry Custard Fool

missed on the last visit. What we do find really useful though is the special children's quiz and trail, as both act as a gentle reminder of what is there, providing elements of the castle's history, its plants and statues. The girls think it very amusing to see their parents trying to answer the questions or forgetting the easiest of answers. However, we always make sure of a return visit to the Clive Museum which is housed in part of what used to be the ballroom, and we always wish we had brushed up on or learnt about Indian history in the days before our visit. And while I like looking at all the military accoutrements including the chain mail armour and the elephant goad, the girls prefer the silver (they are developing extravagant tastes at an early age) – the rosewater sprinklers and the jewelled objects always catch the eye.

The Picnic Site
The designated picnic area overlooking the Italian- and French-inspired herbaceous borders is difficult to beat.

CHEAT'S PICNIC
The restaurant at Powis Castle is worth a visit, not only for its delicious dishes made from locally produced ingredients, but also because it has won the National Trust's top award for quality and service.

ALSO IN THE AREA

● **Chirk Castle, Wrexham** – a magnificent 14th-century fortress overlooking the Marches.

● **Old Oswestry Hill Fort** – an Iron Age fort with really elaborate defences, which provides amazing views across the countryside for miles and miles.

● **Attingham Park, near Shrewsbury** – an elegant Regency manor with deer park and great walks.

● **Erddig, near Wrexham** – a fine 18th-century country house which shows how the servants as well as the family lived. Beautiful parkland with carriage rides available, and demonstrations of restored historic machinery.

● **Benthall Hall and Church, near Ironbridge** – a 16th-century country house and chapel.

● **Ironbridge, Telford** – a World Heritage Site where the world's first ever cast-iron bridge was built over the Severn. Visit the museums and foundries.

Stratford-upon-Avon, Warwickshire
A Day with Will in Shakespeare Country

Stratford-upon-Avon is the most popular tourist destination in the country, after London. That's not really surprising given that it is the birthplace of the world's most famous dramatist, that it is a pretty and historic town which, together with its surroundings offers visitors everything from heritage, culture, arts, gardens and beautiful picnic sites, particularly on the banks of the River Avon. Of course it gets very crowded at the height of the season, so what we like to do is visit either in the spring or early autumn. In fact my favourite time is late summer, early autumn. We also like to get to the town quite early in the day before the bulk of visitors arrive, and wander through the town then, although in the early evening it is also quite nice to sit outside a café, or indeed the riverfront café at the theatre, enjoying a coffee or cold drink, before heading for home. It is endlessly fascinating watching and listening to people who have travelled half way across the world to pay homage to one of our great national treasures and institutions. It makes you very proud and also humble to see how both Shakespeare and his plays are revered from India to Iowa, and I think it is also good for the girls to understand how important the plays and the theatre are to our heritage. As they get older we will visit the theatre more often for matinee performances, having had a wonderful picnic down by the riverside.

My advice is that if you want to explore the town then arrive as early as you can when it is least crowded. We never tire of visiting Shakespeare's birthplace (a tourist attraction for more than 300 years) as well as New Place where he lived after

he made his money, and Nash's House where his granddaughter lived. I am a keen gardener and am particularly fond of the traditional Elizabethan knot garden at New Place.

However our favourite place is Anne Hathaway's Cottage, which is just a short walk from the centre of town, and if we are feeling energetic we will take the footpath from the town centre, although with heavy picnic hampers we usually drive! I heartily recommend the guided tour of the house. But the gardens are magnificent and the maze garden provides an ideal place for a picnic.

The nearby Tree Garden which has examples of all the trees mentioned in the sonnets and plays is great to visit too. It's a good exercise for grown-ups to see how many trees they can identify, but rarely do we get both the tree and the play right. This does, however, stimulate an interest in the children for Shakespeare which pleases me.

We really like walking along the banks of the Avon trying to find the ideal picnic spot. This has such charm, because although we seem to be in the middle of the countryside we really are so close to the centre of the town and everything that is going on there. Next time we plan to hire our own boat and go a little further along the river to find our picnic spot.

ALSO IN THE AREA

● **Mary Arden's House** – Shakespeare's mother's house which is just under five kilometres (three miles) away at Wilmcote. It's got its own farm, Glebe Farm, with livestock, a working blacksmith and a falconry.

● **Charlecote Park** – a beautiful Elizabethan house and deer park which is run by the National Trust, and is where Shakespeare was apparently caught poaching deer.

● **Warwick Castle** – a wonderfully preserved medieval castle which has a number of themed exhibitions, fine grounds and changing exhibitions.

● **Lord Leycester Hospital, Warwick** – an old soldiers' home from the 16th century.

● **The statue of Shakespeare** with four of his best-known characters – Falstaff, Lady Macbeth, Prince Harry and Hamlet – at the Canal Basin where the Stratford-upon-Avon canal meets the Avon. It's a great place for watching narrow boats negotiate the locks.

● **The Falstaff Experience** – at the Shrieves House and Barn in Sheep Street, which is supposed to be the most haunted house in England as 40 individual spirits have been identified. There's a lantern-lit ghost tour at 6pm.

Mansfield, Nottinghamshire
SHERWOOD FOREST AND ROBIN HOOD

One of the great attributes of the British is our need for fair play and our defence of the underdog, and if there is one myth/hero/legend who epitomises this it is Robin Hood, which is why, I imagine, he is so popular with all ages and all genders. In our family, we are all great fans and never tire of the stories, or indeed the films of him. One of our favourites is Disney's *Robin Hood* so we tend to watch the DVD before venturing out for another visit to Sherwood Forest.

It's a spectacular forest covering some 37 acres which became a royal hunting site at the time of the Normans, and now, although it is a fraction of the size it used to be (it was about 100,000 acres, about a fifth of the entire country), it is still impressive and attracts visitors from all over the world – mostly because of that man in green.

Throughout the last millennia the forest has changed and adapted from a huntsman's playground to an outlaw's refuge. The main London to York road, the Great North Road, ran right through the middle of the forest, making it an ideal place from which to rob rich travellers, coaches and carriages while allowing the brigands instant hiding places. And of course, when the wicked Prince John killed Robin of Loxley's father and outlawed our hero, this became the ideal home for him.

It's a good idea to call in at the Visitor Centre first because there is always so much going on and new elements are introduced all the time – from additional marked trails to audio guides to extra information on, and maps of, places of interest, such as Thieves' Wood or the Fountain Dale where Robin first

THE PICNIC

Cheesy Ham Pasties

Apricot and
Pistachio Pilaff

Toffee Apple
Flapjacks

The Picnic Site
Either head for the Sherwood Pine Forest Park where there is ample space for picnics (it is also the start of a number of children's forest trail) or settle down next to the Major Oak and its shady branches.

came across Little John. We love all these stories which somehow seem to sit between fact and fiction, but we don't care – we want to believe these great stories of heroic helpers.

As for the forest itself, apart from its magnificent trees there is myriad wildlife from birds to insects to fruits and flowers, not to mention the grazing herds of cattle and sheep. Of course, it is most famous for its ancient trees – the forestry people say there are 900 trees which are over 600 years old! The most famous of all, the Major Oak, is believed to be almost 1,000 years old, although now it is thought that it might be three or four trees which have fused together. Not surprising, really, when you consider that it weighs an estimated 23 tons and measures 10 metres (33 feet) around the waist – it gives the Chubby Grocer something to aim for!

ALSO IN THE AREA
● **Rufford Abbey and Country Park** – one of the best preserved ruins of a 12th-century Cistercian abbey. The country park has an interesting craft shop, too.
● **Hardwick Hall, near Chesterfield** – one of the grandest and most magnificent Elizabethan houses in existence, built for the doughty Bess of Hardwick. Marvellous pictures and tapestries and a pretty orchard and herb garden.
● **The Workhouse, Southwell** – an insight into another century's version of welfare.
● **Clumber Park, Worksop** – glorious gardens which sport their own miniature Gothic cathedral, the longest avenue of limes in Europe and a varied choice of children's walks, trails and events.
● **Mr Straw's House, Worksop** – a fascinating look at how people lived in the 1920s.

Ripon, North Yorkshire
FOUNTAINS ABBEY AND STUDLEY ROYAL WATER GARDEN

It is impossible not to be awestruck by a visit to the abbey and water garden. In this corner of North Yorkshire, in the Skell valley, sits the grandest and largest monastic ruin in the country, plus 360 acres of a medieval deer park sporting sika, fallow and red deer, a beautiful Victorian church with striking stained glass windows, and a Georgian water garden with ornamental lakes, temples, canals and cascades. One day isn't nearly enough to do justice to this World Heritage Site, and while I am happy to mooch through the 12th-century ruins plus the cellarium and cloisters of the abbey (there is a very good free guided tour), the girls can't wait to run around and explore the vistas and follies of the gardens.

Each time you visit you will come across something you either hadn't seen or noticed before, whether it's among the wealth of statuary (mostly classical gods and heroes), or the lovely temples (one dedicated to Fame, another to Hercules). Then there is the elegance of the Octagon Tower and the sheer

THE PICNIC

Chicken and Garlic Mayo Wraps

Roasted Squash Koftas

Pimm's Jellies

The Picnic Site
Amidst the ruins of the abbey for pure atmosphere, otherwise head for the Temple of Hercules for a cool and shady retreat.

splendour of the lakes stretching across one of the most beautiful of landscapes. The view from the Octagon Tower on its rocky outcrop is worth the effort of trailing through the Serpentine Tunnel, and allows you plenty of time to catch your breath while you admire it.

I think the best plan for the first time visitor is a guided tour in order to get an overall feel of the property, but you can arm yourself with a leaflet of marked walks and peel off whenever you want. There are some great wildlife trails and special ones for children which are fun as well as educational. Fountains Hall itself is a remarkable structure built partly from some of the stones from the ruined abbey. There is no shortage of places in which to enjoy your picnic here, surprising really when you learn that in the 19th century there were strict rules pertaining to visitors who were not allowed to smoke, drink or eat within the property.

CHEAT'S PICNIC

- Farmers' markets are the best places to look for local produce – find them here at Harrogate and Skipton.
- Brymor Ice Cream, High Jervaulx Farm, near Ripon.
- The Swaledale Cheese Co Ltd, near Richmond – award-winning cheese from a recipe dating back to the eleventh century.
- Kettlewell Village Store, near Skipton – traditional village shop with lots of local produce.
- Shepherd's Purse Cheese, Leachfield Grange, near Thirsk – for sheep's milk cheeses.
- The Plough Inn, Wigglesworth – where everything comes from local farmers.

ALSO IN THE AREA

- **Brimham Rocks, Summerbridge** – dramatic rock formations among some 400 acres of woods and moorland.
- **Beningborough Hall and Gardens, York** – beautiful Georgian house with a selection of pictures from the National Portrait Gallery and a great wilderness play area.
- **Spofforth Castle, Harrogate** – visit the ruined hall and chamber of this fortified manor house which once belonged to the all-powerful Percy family.
- **Nunnington Hall, near York** – traditional Yorkshire manor house with impressive organic garden.
- **East Riddlesden Hall, Keighley** – 17th-century manor house, thought to be haunted by myriad apparitions.

Cumbria
THE LAKE DISTRICT

This is one of our all-time favourite places to visit. No matter what time of the year or how long you can stay, there is always something wonderful to see and do. It is, after all, England's largest national park with its highest mountain – Scafell Pike – and deepest lake – Wastwater – as well as 12 of the country's largest lakes and over 3,200 kilometres (2,000 miles) of paths and rights of way.

Every time we decide to visit much discussion takes place on where to go and what to see… and oddly enough the same place keeps cropping up time and time again. The girls (and I mean all three of them) just want to keep going back. It is, of course, Hill Top Farmhouse in Ambleside, where Beatrix Potter lived and wrote many of her books. Weeks before we plan to go, the whole household embarks on what I deem a 'Potterfest' with DVDs and books being watched and pored over – the latest favourite is the new *Miss Potter* film with Renée Zellweger.

However, the house is enchanting, with lots of Beatrix Potter treasures on display, while the farm's vegetable garden is almost exactly as it appears in *Peter Rabbit* and causes huge delight with true Potter fans when they first see it, while some of her original watercolours of it can be seen in the nearby gallery. The farm and the house are incredibly popular so it's best to visit it as early in the day as you can (sadly you can't pre-book tickets, but all are timed) and then, once duty is done, there is all of the amazing Lake Windermere to explore. For it is not all Mrs Tiggy-Winkle and Johnny Town-Mouse – there are

THE PICNIC

Watercress, Carrot, Beetroot and Pine Nut Salad

Thai Pumpkin Soup

Pecan Banana Bread

The Picnic Site
Find a cosy spot on the lakeside at Windermere – there's so much choice. Or take a boat out.

some terrific fell walks nearby and lovely rambles around the lake for all fitness levels. And you can take a boat out on the lake and stop in a remote part for your picnic, or you can just join in one of the very jolly steamer cruises which are on offer.

While it's a place to visit throughout most of the year, the Lake District does tend to get most crowded in summer. My suggestion is to go in spring or autumn as long as you wear warm clothes (layers are best) which can then be popped into a rucksack as the weather brightens and everyone hots up. Spring is particularly famous due to William Wordsworth's *Daffodils*, and a daffodil hunt around the lake will keep everybody warm. However, autumn, when all the leaves are turning gold, red and orange, is amazingly picturesque and is a real treat for any budding photographers in the family.

ALSO IN THE AREA

● **The Peaks** – every bit of land in England over 914 metres (3,000 feet) high is in the Lake District – see how many peaks you can count and with the help of a good map, name them. The highest is Scafell Pike at 978 metres (3,210 feet).

● **It's the ideal day out for nature lovers** with not just the lakes and peaks, but the forests and woods which are home to deer, red squirrels, the only nesting pair of golden eagles in England and mounds of sundew, one of the few carnivorous plants native to Britain.

● **The Lake Poets** – it wasn't just Wordsworth, but Coleridge and Southey also lived here while Shelley, Keats and Tennyson all visited. Back home find one poem from each of these poets to remind you of your day out.

● **Grasmere** – to see Dove Cottage where William Wordsworth lived with his sister, and St. Oswald's churchyard where he is buried.

● **Farming** is one of the main industries in this part of England and Cumbria is famous for its Herdwick sheep, which you can spy throughout the area.

● **Mining, especially Honister mine** – for many years copper, lead, graphite and slate mining were carried out in the region and it is possible to spot old mines. Slate mining still takes place at Honister mines, while graphite mining led to the development of the pencil industry.

● **Muncaster Castle, Gardens and Owl Centre** – magnificent gardens, great plant centre and wondrous owl collection.

CHEAT'S PICNIC

● **The George Hotel, Orton** – serves mainly local produce and is an avid supporter of the award-winning local farmers' market (if your visit is on the second Saturday of the month, the market is a great treat).

● **Tower Bank Arms, near to Hill Top** – also owned by the National Trust and serves traditional Cumbrian dishes using local produce.

● **Orton and Pooley Bridge Farmers' Market**, for suppliers such as: Think Drink– apple juice; Broughton Village Bakery – great bread, quiche, etc.; Swaledale Cheese Company; Country Fare – cakes and gingerbread; Wooden Spoon Fudge; Cumberland Sausage Company; Gingerbread from the Grasmere Gingerbread shop; Kendal Mint Cake – great for energy on long walks.

Holy Island, Northumberland
LINDISFARNE

This is an extraordinary day out with much to see and experience. However, the tides decide exactly how long you can remain on the island, so the first thing you must do is check the time of the tides. Driving across the causeway to the island you begin to realise just how special this place is, for suddenly in front of you is the castle, at first seemingly rising on a great rock from the sea, while way in the distance you can spot the rainbow arch of the priory. I always notice how the voices inside the car get quieter as we get nearer.

THE PICNIC

Goats' Cheese with Basil and Sweet Chilli Sauce

Marinated Beef with Roasted Cherry Tomatoes

Melon and Mint Crush

In good weather Lindisfarne is one of the most beautiful places on earth, but even when it clouds over it is still awe-inspiring. I suggest arriving as early as possible, not just to have sufficient time on the island, but also to ensure a good place in the car park (however, if you decide to curtail your stay your parking ticket can be used in a number of neighbouring towns, such as Berwick and Wooler). A quick visit to the Lindisfarne Centre is certainly useful because that's where you discover what is new, which exhibitions are open and what changes, if any, there have been since your last visit.

It is astonishing to realise that this tiny tidal island is so important in the history of this country, and is probably the holiest of Anglo-Saxon sites. And when you look out onto the vastness and bleakness of the North Sea, you wonder what brought that Irish monk St. Aidan here 14 centuries ago. But then when you turn and look at the Northumbrian coast, you see little but beauty and begin to understand the slightly mystical and spiritual qualities of the place. Its name, Lindisfarne, means 'Land's Corner', underlining the fact that you really are in a very special corner of England.

The priory ruins and its museum are an absolute must, in fact the latter is one of the best I've been to. Standing among the ruins, listening to wind and the birdsong is a truly uplifting, and calming, experience – and you wonder how the monks must have felt in such an exposed location as wave after wave of Viking marauders arrived. The castle is a much more comforting experience with its 16th-century exterior and its fine 20th-century

The Picnic Site
Find a sheltered spot on the coast with a stone wall acting as a natural windbreaker at your back, or among the ruins of the priory in a quiet, secluded spot.

Lutyens-designed interiors. We are very keen on the walled garden, which was designed and planted by the incomparable Gertrude Jekyll and always hope we will be there on a day when there is a plant sale!

But best of all we like to find some sheltered spot which allows us spectacular views of the castle and the sea, and with some luck a good sighting of grey seals, playing in the waves or sleeping on the rocks.

CHEAT'S PICNIC

● **Heatherslaw Bakery, Cornhill on Tweed** – for breads, cakes and biscuits.
● **Chain Bridge Honey Farm, Berwick upon Tweed** – for local honeys.
● **Doddington Dairy** – delicious cheeses and ice cream.
● **The Cheese Shop, Morpeth** – for local cheeses from Blagdon and Doddington.
● **The Proof of the Pudding, Alnwick** – sticky toffee, chocolate and ginger puddings and sauces.
● And, of course, **mead from Lindisfarne**.

ALSO IN THE AREA

● **Bamburgh Castle** – magnificent and imposing, it dominates the coast and the site has been occupied since prehistoric times. Often considered the finest castle in England.
● **The Farne Islands** – great for seal spotting and bird watching, particularly puffins, kittiwakes and terns.
● **Dunstanburgh Castle** – huge ruined castle with impressive views across the sea and along the coast.
● **Alnwick** – (pronounced 'annick')a charming market town with cobbled streets and square, and Alnwick Castle with its Canalettos and other old masters.
● **Warkworth Castle and Hermitage** – home of Shakespeare's Harry Hotspur and one of the largest and most impressive fortresses in the north. The Hermitage can only be accessed by boat across the river Coquet.
● **Norham Castle** – one of the strongest of the border castles and frequently attacked by the Scots, especially Robert Bruce.

Kelso, Roxburgh
FLOORS CASTLE

This is undoubtedly one of the UK's prettiest castles in the most picturesque of settings in the Scottish Borders – little wonder it has been used in a number of films and TV programmes, including *Greystoke – the Legend of Tarzan*.

Built for the first Duke of Roxburghe by William Adam, possibly to a design by Sir John Vanbrugh, it sits overlooking the valley of the Tweed, surrounded by some beautiful parkland and gardens. And while I love the trees (there is a spectacular collection at Floors, with some very old oaks and limes), Judith is a great enthusiast of the parterre which was planted to mark the Millennium as well as the Walled Garden, where Queen Victoria once stopped for tea. Her favourite part is the tunnel of colour and scent, a riot of shades and fragrance, while the girls always have fun in the adventure playground.

But first of all we have to do a tour of the house – simply because there is always something different to see and learn. The guides have known the house, and the family, for years and have a fund of stories which

THE PICNIC

Hearty Sausage and Barley Soup

Italian Picnic Pasties

Plum Crumble Squares with Cinnamon

The Picnic Site
At the special picnic area on the edge of the woodland with gentle views over the River Tweed.

makes each visit quite unique. Even though it is a castle, and the rooms are vast and filled with amazing antiques, because it has been in the same family since it was built it really does feel like a home.

Whenever we are heading for Scotland we always make a little detour to visit Floors. A walk by the River Tweed is not just a way of working up an appetite, it is also a great place to spot herons and oyster catchers – gradually every member of the family is becoming an amateur twitcher and there is much competition to see who spots which type of bird, first. We invariably call in at the Terrace Café for coffee or a cold drink, and then we stock up on pickles and preserves, all prepared by the castle chef, to bring home, as well as some freshly made bread or cakes to add to our picnic.

ALSO IN THE AREA
● **Jedburgh Abbey** – a marvellous ruined 12th-century Augustinian abbey.
● **Mellerstain House, Gordon** – one of Scotland's great Georgian houses which was begun in 1725 by William Adam and completed several years later by his famous son, Robert.
● **Abbotsford House** – the home of Sir Walter Scott with masses of the writer's memorabilia, lovely grounds and a fine river walk overlooking the Tweed. There's a good café too.
● **Dryburgh Abbey** – hidden away due to a wide loop in the River Tweed, these medieval ruins highlight its seclusion as well as its spirituality.
● **Priorwood Garden and Dried Flower Shop** – charming garden where plants are chosen specifically for their drying qualities. An enthusiast's view of paradise. Lovely orchard which cultivates historic apple varieties.

GAZETTEER

Planning routes these days is pretty straightforward – no more enormous maps on your knees! If you have a satellite navigation system in your car just pop in the postcodes below. Alternatively, go to my website www.chubbygrocerpicnics.co.uk and click on the directions link.

CHELTENHAM RACES: OLD GLOUCESTER RD, ANDOVERSFORD	GL54 4HR
DARTMOOR: MINIATURE PONY CENTRE	TG13 BRG
BOX HILL	KT20 7LB
BROWNSEA ISLAND	BH13 7EE
DOVER	CT16 1HJ
FLOORS CASTLE	TD5 7SF
FOUNTAINS ABBEY	HG4 3DY
HAY-ON-WYE: CHURCH ST	HR3 5DQ
HILL TOP	LA22 5DQ
JURASSIC COAST: THE COBB, LYME REGIS	DT7 3JF
LINDISFARNE: VISITORS' CENTRE	TD15 2SD
LONGSTOCK WATER GARDENS	SO20 6JF
PANGBOURNE: HIGH ST	RG1 2EG
POWIS CASTLE	LD6 5DL
SHERWOOD FOREST COUNTRY PARK	NG21 9HN
STRATFORD-UPON-AVON: ROYAL SHAKESPEARE THEATRE	CV37 6BB
STONEHENGE	SN8 1RF
TURVILLE: THE BULL AND BUTCHER	RG9 6QU

INDEX

spinach, Parmesan and spaghetti
    frittata 35
squash: koftas, roasted 58
roasted vegetable salad 78
strawberries: Bakewell tart 122
    Eton mess 112
sweet potato: in empanadas 34

tart, savoury: bacon and pea 69
    goat's cheese and pesto 45
    leek and Cheddar 40
    onion and Gruyère 51
tart, sweet: cherry and almond 130
    strawberry Bakewell 122
Thai pumpkin soup 102
tomatoes: cherry, roasted 74
    in Italian picnic pasties 73
    in pitta pockets 19
tortilla, vegetable 41

trout, hot-smoked, and leek
frittata 56
twists, Parmesan 50
tzatziki 42

vegetable: and bean soup 104
    and feta parcels 46
    roasted, in salads 78, 87
    tortilla, Spanish 41
vinaigrette, saffron 98

warmers (drinks) 144–5
watercress: pesto 83
    in pitta pockets 19
    poached salmon with 54
    in salad 80
wraps: chicken and garlic mayo 25
    hummus, corn and beetroot 16

ACKNOWLEDGEMENTS

In true Oscar style, I need to begin with my parents, without whom the world of picnics would be lifeless. My brother Stuart and sister Colette were willing participants in picnic play in woods, paddling pools or the beach, and I have many happy memories of our time together. For the last 20 years my wonderful wife, Judith, and my daughters, Holly and Lily, have been the best of outdoor companions and this book is dedicated to them.

I would also single out Jo Foley, Jan Maish and Lisa Whitehouse for helping put the book together, and to Waitrose for advising on the wonderful recipes, to Sara Pearson for getting it off the ground, and my brilliant PA Zoë for all her help.

To Peter Cameron for helping me build the Chubby Grocer Picnics website so that everyone can share their favourite picnic adventures.

Lastly, I want to credit the great British countryside. In my opinion, there is no more beautiful country in the world. And to help preserve and protect it, all my profits from this book will be donated to The National Trust.

1 3 5 7 9 10 8 6 4 2

Published in 2008 by Ebury Press, an imprint of Ebury Publishing

A Random House Group Company

The Random House Group Limited Reg. No. 954009

Addresses for companies within the Random House Group can be found at
www.randomhouse.co.uk

A CIP catalogue record for this book is available from the British Library

The Random House Group Limited supports The Forest Stewardship Council (FSC),
the leading international forest certification organisation. All our titles that are printed on
Greenpeace approved FSC certified paper carry the FSC logo. Our paper
procurement policy can be found at www.rbooks.co.uk/environment

To buy books by your favourite authors and register for offers visit www.rbooks.co.uk

Design: Two Associates
Food photography: Will Heap
Recipe Editor: Nicola Graimes
Food stylist: Cara Hobday
Props stylist: Tessa Evelegh

Rugs kindly loaned by Melin Tregwynt, Castlemorris, Haverfordwest, Pembrokeshire SA62 5UX
Mail order tel: 01348 891 644; www.melintregwynt.co.uk

Printed and bound in Italy by Printer Trento

ISBN 9780091927073